W9-COD-645

Whitetail Wisdom

Hunting Wisdom Library™

MINNETONKA, MINNESOTA

About the Editors

GORDY KRAHN is editor of *North American Hunter* magazine. Whitetail pursuits have taken him across North America, always with a passion for the hunt and an eye toward strategies, techniques and tips for success.

TOM CARPENTER is creative director at the North American Hunting Club. He has written about whitetails for many years, hunted them for even more, and edited multiple books on the pursuit of our favorite big game animal.

WHITETAIL WISDOM

Printed in 2011.

Tom Carpenter
Creative Director

Jen Weaverling
Managing Editor

Wendy Holdman
Book Design and Production

4 5 6 7 8 9 10 / 14 13 12 11

© 2009 North American Hunting Club

ISBN 10: 1-58159-453-4
ISBN 13: 978-1-58159-453-9

North American Hunting Club
12301 Whitewater Drive
Minnetonka, Minnesota 55343
www.huntingclub.com

PHOTO CREDITS

Grady Allen: 58, 59; **Charles Alsheimer:** 4, 6, 13, 17, 43, 46, 47, 55, 70, 72, 73, 90, 107, 119, 140, 149; **Scott Anderson:** 12 (4); **Mike Barlow/Windigoimages:** 23, 94; **Shane Benoit:** 98, 99, **Mike Bigs:** 129; **Boone and Crockett Club** (Old Milwaukee Depot, 250 Station Drive, Missoula, MT 59801-2753): 122; **Brian P. Bower:** 88, 92; **Denver Bryan:** 100; **Bill Buckley/THE GREEN AGENCY:** 45, 113, 132; **Jim Casada:** 64 (4); **Tom Carpenter/North American Hunting Club:** 2, 26; **Dawn Charging:** 5; **Tim Christie:** 89, 153; **Gary Clancy:** 82, 83, 85; **Judd Cooney/Windigoimages:** 73, 139; **Laurie Lee Dovey:** 77; **Denny Eilers/Windigoimages:** 85; **Betty Lou Fegely:** 2, 101; **Tom Fegely:** onlay, 33, 37; **John Ford:** 50, 130, 150; **M.H. Francis:** 131; **Russel Graves/Windigoimages:** 80; **Larry Holjencin:** 20, 71, 113, 114, 115 (6); **Donald M. Jones:** 21, 62, 74, 86; **Mark Kayser:** 28, 96, 112, 125; **Mitch Keyzar/Windigoimages:** 25, 138; **Bill Kinney:** 1, 8, 38, 60, 87, 91, 102, 103, 104, 106, 118, 123, 126, 127, 128, 148, 156; **Gordy Krahn:** 2, 83; **Lance Krueger:** 111; **Lon E. Lauber/Windigoimages:** 64, 68, 109, 139; **Bill Lea:** 32, 34, 44, 64, 116, 117; **Bruce Leventhal/Windigoimages:** 138; **Dave Maas/North American Hunting Club:** 15, 19, 59; **Bill Marchel/Windigoimages:** 22, 24 (2), 25, 54, 93, 95, 118; **Ian McMurchy:** 51; **Bill Miller/North American Hunting Club:** 5; **Mark Palas/Windigoimages:** 130; **Dean Pearson/Windigoimages:** 137, 138; **Mark Raycroft:** 120; **Jack Rodgers:** 141, 142; **Glenn Sapir:** 144, 145, 147; **Richard P. Smith:** 65; **Bryce Towsley:** 97, 98; **Larry Weishuhn:** 36; **Grant Woods:** 16, 18.

ILLUSTRATIONS

Chris Armstrong: 10-11, 40-41, 48-49, 52-53, 66-67, 83, 84, 134-135, 154-155; **C. J. Winand:** 56 (both).

Table of Contents

Foreword

Photographs, mounts and memories are all wonderful things. Each of them reminds you of days when everything went right. Each of them is proof that at least once you had a trophy buck under your spell, instead of vice versa. Each of them can last beyond the hunter's lifetime, when cared for and shared.

Whitetail wisdom is the result of that kind of success and, perhaps even more so, of failure. The truly wise hunter learns from his or her mistakes.

Yet for most of us, that kind of wisdom is too hard won. More than anything else, true whitetail wisdom is gained only through contacts with deer — many contacts, hundreds of contacts, thousands of contacts — the more contacts the greater the wisdom. Unfortunately, that leaves most of us holding the short end of the stick when it comes to amassing a personal horde of whitetail wisdom. How many professional hunters and wildlife research biologists can the world support? Somebody in this world needs to cut meat. Somebody has to make bread. Somebody's got to run the lighting design store downtown.

But the butchers, the bakers and the candlestick makers are hunters too. And they want whitetail wisdom, though they can't always go out and spend the time it takes to create their own. So to make up for the time they can't spend in the field, they collect the vicarious knowledge of expert hunters and whitetail researchers. Folks like writer and biologist Larry Weishuhn, who authors *North American Hunter's* "Whitetails" column in each issue of the magazine. Folks like Dr. Grant Woods, who has devoted his life and career to expanding the understanding of North America's most popular big game animal. Folks like Charlie Alsheimer, who spends weeks on end in the woods with camera as well as gun and bow to participate in the whitetails' secret ceremonies. Folks like North American Hunting Club's team of professional editors and TV producers.

That's why their stories, originally published in *North American Hunter* magazine, along with the works of many more expert hunters and deer behaviorists, are included in this special NAHC edition. They are offering to share with you their hard-won, lifelong collection of "Whitetail Wisdom." The North American Hunting Club is proud to play this role in helping you make these undeniable experts' wisdom your very own!

Enjoy *Whitetail Wisdom . . .* and good hunting.

Bill

Bill Miller
Executive Director — North American Hunting Club

Introduction

Welcome to the world of the white-tailed deer.
Step inside, shed your blaze orange and warm your hands as you page through the most powerful collection of whitetail hunting information and photography ever produced by the North American Hunting Club. That's right. You're holding the best of the best, written and photographed by some of the best in the business.

And this business of whitetail hunting is a serious matter. For many of us, the whitetail is the big game animal. It's quite likely the first big game animal you ever hunted, and, for some of us, it will be the only big-game animal we ever pursue. Many of us live and die deer hunters. You may have had the good fortune to match wits with a variety of big-game species, but most of us could be quite satisfied with nothing but whitetail adventures on our hunting horizons.

Challenge? There's not an animal better equipped to elude a hunter. Terrain? You'll find bucks clinging to steep slopes in the Rockies, dashing across grasslands in Kansas, running Pennsylvania ridges and skulking in Mississippi swamps. Excitement? If you've ever had a mature buck come to the sound of rattling antlers, a grunt call or a decoy, you've had one of the finest big-game hunting experiences North America has to offer.

Most of us grew up with whitetails and took our first deer after a few years of hope-filled effort. There have been many deer since, but we still thrill to the sound of crunching leaves in autumn woods. Many of us live for bowhunting the bucks of our dreams. We still cross off calendar days as the firearms opener approaches, and we dream of a cabin, camper, tent camp, farm or other wonderful place where family and old friends gather each fall. And we still hate to leave the deer woods when the season ends.

May you enjoy this book and your days with the white-tailed deer. And no matter where deer trails lead you this fall, may the words and images from these pages go with you.

Good hunting!

CHAPTER 1

Whitetail Management

Science? Management? Deer hunting is much more art than science, yet what dedicated deer hunter doesn't crave new scientific research on antler growth or quality deer management? *North American Hunter*'s "Whitetails" columnist, Larry Weishuhn — also known as "Mr. Whitetail" — talks with thousands of deer hunters each year at seminars. He also reaches millions through the many whitetail articles he writes. If there's one area of whitetail hunting Larry keeps getting questions about, it's really not about the "hunting" part at all. It's about producing more mature bucks.

Proper deer management (improving habitat, harvest strategies and genetics) can mean healthier herds and bucks with bigger antlers. Any veteran whitetail hunter knows that he or she cannot consistently take large bucks in areas lacking in quality habitat or management practices. The best rattling, grunt calls or stand locations won't put you in range of a Boone-and-Crockett-class buck in South Carolina, for example, or even in parts of states like Minnesota, Pennsylvania, Michigan or Texas. The bottom line is that, for a number of reasons, there are areas (even in some of the best states) that don't produce huge bucks. Thus, a great many great deer hunters never kill a "great" deer by record-book standards.

That might not matter a whole lot to you. But for many hunters, it would be nice to think that dream could become reality. And proper management isn't just about producing big bucks. It's about doe harvests and keeping populations in check. It's about finding creative ways to deal with deer in urban areas.

Let's find out more . . .

■ ■ ■

Prime Property

LARRY WEISHUHN

Mine, all mine! How often have you looked at deer habitat and wished you owned or had complete control of that piece of property? Let's imagine that whitetail heaven on earth was yours. You determine who has permission to hunt, how many and what type of deer are harvested, and what habitat improvements to make for the deer and other wildlife.

Wouldn't that be great?

In a way, I gained ownership to a prime piece of deer hunting property overnight when *North American Hunter*'s managing editor approached me at the Shooting, Hunting and Outdoor Trade (SHOT) Show. He presented the question and the story assignment. "What would you do if you were given title to 640 acres of land and wanted to improve it for white-tailed deer and deer hunting? You decide where it's located and tell the North American Hunting Club members what you would do with it, Mr. Whitetail."

I thought about it for a few moments as my mind already started racing with food plots and deer management strategies. I finally replied that I'd love to give it a go, but I knew this story wouldn't be easy.

For years I've managed large properties for white-tailed deer. During that time I've helped to establish quality wildlife management programs on more than 15 million acres. This work has helped me gain valuable insight into maintaining healthy deer herds. But helping a rancher in Texas manage 20,000 acres is a lot different than helping the average NAHC member improve his Back 40, if he's fortunate enough to own even 40 acres. But as access to hunting property gets tougher, more deer hunters are looking for land of their own. This story is meant to help illustrate what to look for and how to maximize the potential of that deer habitat.

I'd prefer a square piece of property or as close to square as possible. I'd also want "my land" situated between similar-sized properties and not bordered on more than one side by a public road. Ideally, this region would be blessed with fertile soil and sufficient rainfall to produce native browse and forage crops. One or more small creek bottoms with mast-producing trees

would be excellent. If the country has a reputation for producing massive, long-tined bucks, that's icing on the cake. Western Kentucky, northern Missouri and southern Iowa would be some of my top choices. I've hunted whitetails in each location and drooled over properties I'd dearly love to own.

AN ACTION PLAN

After spending a little time on the property to get a feel for it, my first step would be to gather as much information about it as possible. I want to know about past hunting and agricultural practices (which I'll assume amounted to some farming and grazing by livestock). I'd try to find out how my neighbors hunt whitetails.

Deer Desert to Whitetail Wonderland

I t's a couple thousand acres of soybeans, corn, alfalfa and oak ridges littered with acorns. A whitetail paradise in a place where a deer sighting was big news just over a decade ago.

But excellent habitat isn't the only ingredient in a program aimed at producing quality bucks. Scott Anderson, owner of Backland Camo, has joined in an effort with a southern Minnesota farmer to improve the property for whitetails.

"I went down turkey hunting 10 years ago, and there were just a few deer," Anderson says. "It's mostly a landowner willing to sacrifice some crops for the wildlife."

Mineral sites (like the before-and-after examples in the top two photos), food plots, nitrogen treatments for mast-producing trees, designated sanctuary areas and a new deer harvest mentality have combined to produce impressive results (as seen in the bottom two photos).

Anderson arrowed the record-book whitetail (third photo from top) in mid-October. A week later, Gregg Gutschow joined Anderson and took the eight-point at right. Both bucks field-dressed in excess of 200 pounds. In terms of antler size, however, Gutschow's buck would be considered just over the minimum for harvest in most quality deer management programs.

Scott Anderson's son, Chad, empties a bottle of mineral-vitamin supplement and returns a few weeks later to see how much the deer like this spot. You can see some of the results below.

Our hypothetical plot of 640 acres is a good-sized parcel, but most whitetails will roam over a larger expanse of land. Neighboring hunting practices would determine where I would establish food plots and habitat improvements.

Let's make some additional assumptions. First, I received the property in January. The year before, about 200 acres were in crops. The remaining 440 acres consists of woods interspersed with small fields. These small fields might have been farmed years ago, but now they're grown up in native weeds and shrubs.

My next step would be to contact a neighboring farmer to see if he'd be interested in leasing my cropland. In the lease agreement, there would be a stipulation that he plant only crops that I approved of — primarily corn, soybeans and alfalfa. Secondly, I would insist that he leave 15 to 20 rows of the crops standing in the fields along the brushlines. From there,

I'd try to make an arrangement with him to plant my smaller food plots with seeds that I provide. Tractors and equipment are extremely expensive, and I see no reason to own this machinery unless you're a farmer. However, a four-wheel-drive ATV would be a real asset on our property.

The farmer and I would also discuss where to plant the various crops in the existing fields and how to clear strips in the grown-over fields where I'd like to have alfalfa planted. Some strips should also be "bush-hogged" or shredded using a tractor and mower to lower the level of the plants while maintaining the root system. This should happen in late winter — as soon as the snow is gone. In spring or early summer, we would plant the alfalfa. I prefer alfalfa rather than other legumes because there are varieties of alfalfa adapted to different areas, seed sources are readily available and relatively inexpensive, it is a proven producer of quality forage, and deer love the stuff.

Throughout spring and summer, my goal would be to produce as much quality browse and forage for the deer as possible. I'd want some of that forage to be available during winter. In most of the whitetail's habitat, the two major nutritional stress periods are late summer and winter. To produce a healthy deer herd, these are the times you need to ensure sufficient quantity and quality of food — focus on the interior of the property. As a matter of fact, the majority of my habitat improvements would be at the center of the property if possible.

In addition to the farm crops in the existing fields, food plots and strips, I'd establish mineral licks in the wooded areas near the center of the property. Provided this is legal in the state where I own this land, I'd dig shallow depressions and bait those areas with corn or mistletoe because I want the deer to know there is something special about that exact location. Once they start coming to those spots, I'd switch from the corn or mistletoe to a mineral/vitamin supplement. Deer will indeed use mineral supplements either in block or granular form when they are available, especially in late spring and early summer. A little corn or mistletoe on top wouldn't hurt. Every other month or so, I'd replenish the mineral/vitamin supplement. On the 640 acres, I'd want 10 to 15 of the sites, but I'd have no intention of hunting near any of them.

■■■

"The majority of my habitat improvements would be at the center of my property."

■■■

To improve the nutrients in and quantity of the plants growing on my property, I'd use food-plot growth enhancers. Some of the better products on the market include ingredients such as gibberellic acid, kinetin and butyric acid derivatives. These products can be used when planting, after plants have sprouted and during maturity to help stimulate root growth and improve the plant's metabolism, which will increase yields.

Furthermore, most products have been developed to the point where they are compatible with a wide range of vegetation and soil consistencies. When used during planting of other vegetation, like trees and shrubs, today's enhancers can reduce natural mortality by up to 40 percent.

Don't confuse growth enhancers with fertilizer. In fact, enhancers will actually help plants efficiently use fertilizers that might be applied to fields, food plots or natural browse. They also make the browse much more palatable; thus deer tend to feed on treated plants more readily.

I mentioned that the property would have some mast-producing trees. Fall mast crops are extremely important in places that experience harsh winters because nuts, like acorns, are high in fat and carbohydrates and help whitetails add fat. Many mast and fruit trees do not produce every year. However, production can be increased with other commercial enhanc-

ers. Several manufacturers offer these "root gel" type products. These gels and sprays are usually diluted with water and are then applied around the edge of the dripline (after the leaves have been cleared from the application area) of mast and fruit trees. This will help ensure more consistent mast production. I would apply growth enhancers to selected trees throughout the property, but especially in those areas that I planned to hunt later in fall.

As a final ingredient to enhancing the health of the plants, deer and other wildlife on my property, I'd fertilize with 13-13-13 in the same areas that I used enhancers. This fertilizer includes 13 percent nitrogen, 13 percent phosphorus and 13 percent potash.

EVALUATING AND ADJUSTING

Whenever I'm on the property, I'll maintain a journal of where I find shed antlers, buck rubs or scrapes. I'll also make notes of the individual deer I see and try to recognize bucks that I'll identify by antler characteristics. In spring I'll want to try to gauge how many fawns were born on the property. In summer I'd contact the local game warden or state wildlife biologist and ask him to assist me in setting up a nighttime spotlight game survey on my property. If this is illegal in my area, I'd request that the state wildlife department conduct the survey. What I'm looking for is an estimated population and composition of the deer herd. Only with this information can I or a deer biologist determine how many does and bucks should be harvested. This survey would be done annually.

Food plots are always important deer management components.

Small-Scale Management Can Produce Big Results

by NAHC Member Ada Klute

Our hunting spot in southern Wisconsin is typical farmland whitetail country — rolling fields mixed with small woodlots. Heavy hunting pressure exists on surrounding properties, and most hunters stand by their traditional buck-only hunting.

My husband, Kevin, and I decided to do what we could to improve our odds of seeing more deer and producing better bucks on our farm. We don't have a lot of land, but we wanted to try anyway. This plan started over a decade ago, and we've experimented by trial and error.

The logical place to start was with the habitat on our property. Our 40 acres of cropland is managed to provide some feed for the deer. The hay is cut twice a season. This leaves 8- to 12-inch clover/alfalfa mix standing during fall and winter. Corn is picked to leave the stubble high and some cobs scattered about. We also plant several types of food plots.

In the 80 acres of woods, we attempt to offer forage and security cover. Each spring we plant trees and shrubs that are not native to our area but are preferred browse species for whitetails. The rest of the year is spent removing unwanted trees. By dropping these trees, thick patches of cover are instantly created. The deer also browse the fallen tops, and the increased amount of sun reaching the forest floor stimulates new plant growth.

We also maintain mineral licks all year. To help the deer stay healthy through the winter, we plant late-season food plots.

We didn't expect any miracles to happen overnight, but we could see small improvements each year. We went from rare sightings of bucks during bow and gun seasons to seeing several different yearling bucks during that same time span. Our next progression in this new management philosophy was to try to produce more mature, large-antlered bucks.

That required a change in our approach to hunting. So we reduced the hunting pressure on our property.

"We never dreamed of being able to hunt such big bucks, and there are bigger ones out there."

Deer drives were eliminated. Today, only four hunters are allowed during gun season, with at least 40 acres of woods set aside as a sanctuary. We even have cooling-off days where no one hunts.

During the lengthy bow season, Kevin and I practice a similar low-pressure strategy. We made a rule that any buck you shoot must be larger than the last one you took with that hunting tool. No exceptions. This has eliminated low-percentage shots and challenged us and other hunters on the property to let deer get closer for better inspection. It also makes for more exciting hunting. There is the potential for a few buck-less seasons because of this rule. But the freezer is always filled with fresh venison since we have plenty of antlerless-only tags to cull adult does. We take extra caution to make sure no one mistakenly harvests a buck fawn.

By selectively harvesting deer in this way, we have witnessed a more defined rut. Mature bucks are now more prevalent, improving our hunting and the quality of the local deer herd.

Firearms deer season is now a lot more enjoyable for us. It's not uncommon to have up to 30 does and fawns feeding in our fields during legal shooting hours. The real thrill is when a couple of bucks (some of them real dandies) are out there with them. These deer don't even seem to realize that the firearms season is going on.

During bow season, we're almost guaranteed to see deer on every outing. One morning I saw 11 different bucks while I was on stand. That was more bucks in one morning than I had seen in 10 years of hunting the old way.

The surrounding hunters used to think we were nuts for letting a buck go. It's been a lot of hard work, but we believe it's been worth it. We never dreamed of being able to hunt such big bucks, and there are bigger ones out there. We only wish we could have had all this knowledge back when we bought our farm.

Creating openings like this with adjoining security cover promotes use by whitetails.

In this scenario, let's say that after several surveys we determine that there are approximately 80 deer on my 640 acres. Sufficient food now exists on this land even during the hard times. Let's also assume that this is the approximate number of deer I'd like to maintain on the property — at least until I can increase the carrying capacity. Let's say that the survey showed that 15 of the 80 deer are bucks, 40 are does and 25 are fawns. These numbers would indicate, to me at least, an over-harvest of bucks and a lack of proper nutrition during the hard months, given the low 60 percent fawn survival rate.

That first year I'd only take one buck — and only if it's a real dandy. I want to improve the buck-to-doe ratio and fawn recruitment. Thus, the family and friends can come out and shoot does on any hunting tags that would allow the harvest of antlerless deer. Tagging 10 does would be my goal the first fall.

Now the property has 14 bucks, 30 does and 25 fawns; about half of the fawns would be bucks. The following fall my survey shows that the property holds approximately 23 bucks (some of the young bucks wander off and do not return), 40 does and 30 fawns. That fall my harvest goals would be two bucks and 15 does (essentially taking the number of doe fawns being brought into the herd by reproduction). The third fall's survey estimates 35 bucks, 50 does and 50 fawns on my land. That hunting season my family and friends and I will shoot for 10 bucks (five mature bucks and five with undesirable antler characteristics) and 30 does. By the fourth fall, the deer herd stands at 40 bucks, 45 does and 40 fawns.

THE END RESULT

Now, each fall I'll hope to harvest 15 bucks and 20 to 25 does, exact numbers depending upon the fawn crop. Natural mortality, predation and yearling dispersion are also going to take some animals each year. With a good hunting program, natural mortality should be minimal. By the fifth year, I should have been able to increase the food supply greatly and, thus, the carrying capacity of the habitat on my property. With the described hunting practices, the average age of the bucks should also have increased.

I'm a stickler on keeping records. I'd record weight, age and antler measurements of every deer taken. Only through good records can any program truly be evaluated. An important side benefit of all this habitat work is that all the rest of the wildlife benefits as well.

First and foremost, though, as stated at the start of this piece, is improving my land for whitetails. As you can see, it requires an equal amount of habitat work and herd management. That means proper harvest levels of bucks and does as I've often preached. I get great pleasure from seeing results on property that I manage. If you're a landowner and a deer hunter, I think you'll experience similar gratification. And one thing's for certain. You'll learn more about deer than you ever knew before. And, once again, that's what the science of deer hunting is all about.

A Hunger for Deer Food

DR. GRANT WOODS

EDITOR'S NOTE: *Food plots are great tools to increase the quality and quantity of forage available for wildlife. They can also significantly increase the opportunity to observe most species of game animals. However, some sportsmen have experienced frustration and limited success with their attempts to establish and maintain food plots. This story by Dr. Grant Woods, a consulting research wildlife biologist, is aimed at assisting North American Hunting Club members in preparing and benefiting from a successful food plot program.*

Simply put, food plots are areas where vegetation is established and maintained in an effort to attract wildlife and provide nutritious forage for selected game species. But devising an effective food plot strategy that will deliver maximum results is a challenge that hunters and biologists are keenly interested in. Sportsmen and women commonly create food plots for several species of wildlife including deer, turkeys, doves and quail. This story will focus on the use of food plots for management of white-tailed deer, even though most species of game will benefit from what we plant.

Why are food plots so important for management of white-tailed deer? There are several important reasons. The first relates to deer feeding habits. Whitetails are very selective feeders and will consistently feed in the area of their home range where the most palatable food source exists. Deer will often pass up abundant supplies of less palatable forage to feed on a more tasty food source. These habits can be a tremendous advantage to anyone trying to observe or harvest whitetails. For example, many knowledgeable hunters select stand locations near white oak trees, knowing that deer prefer the sweeter white oak acorns over the bitter acorns of red oaks.

Biologists often refer to choice, nutritious deer forage as "ice cream" foods because of their strong attracting capabilities. By creating food plots, sportsmen can control where palatable food sources are located. And this can be used to the sportsman's advantage, influencing where deer will feed and the corridors they will choose to travel to and from feeding areas.

The second and more important management aspect of food plots relates to nutrition. And this is what most of us, hunters and biologists alike, are interested in. Most deer herds

Many food plot seed types are available, but all fall into annual or perennial categories. Consult a local farmer or agricultural extension agent on which varieties might flourish where you hunt.

Protein means antlers like these on this healthy buck. Does and fawns rely on nutritious forage, too.

across the country today do not receive optimum nutrition. The rapidly expanding white-tailed deer population in most areas has compounded the problem. But planting the appropriate forage species can significantly increase the quantity and quality of nutritious browse. This is critical if the goal is to increase the number and/ or quality of deer on your property.

Why is nutrition so important for white-tailed deer? Beyond the basic issues of general health, nutrition is critical to bucks for growing antlers and to does for reproduction. A buck converts some of the energy he consumes into the production of antlers. If a buck is to express the antler growth potential for his age, he must have a diet of digestible forage that contains 16 percent or more protein. Forage tests of common native browse species show that they usually contain only seven to 13 percent protein. This means that most bucks across the country would grow larger antlers if their protein intake were increased. Likewise, does require optimal nutrition to conceive twins each year. If a doe's nutritional intake is insufficient, she might bear a single fawn or none at all.

■■■

"If you don't live in an area with a lot of agriculture, food plots are a great tool to improve the quality of a deer herd."

■■■

Planted food sources benefit whitetails because they generally offer far more protein and nutrition than native browse. Food plots also increase the quantity of available forage on a per-acre basis. Native browse species generally produce only 100 to 500 pounds of digestible forage per acre annually, compared to food plots, where production often tops 10,000 pounds per acre. The bottom line is that bucks will not develop their full antler potential, and does will not reach their reproductive potential, without a sustained supply of quality forage. Food plots are an excellent way to meet the demand.

Within any large area, the biggest deer of each age class will be found where the most nutritious and digestible forage is. For this reason, in areas where the herd was stocked from the same source, farmland deer generally have bigger antlers and are more productive compared to deer of the same age class living in areas where agricultural crops are limited. Missouri, where I grew up hunting, is a perfect example. The northern half of the state is composed of intensive agriculture while the southern half is almost exclusively timbered, with a mix of habitat types in the middle.

Antler development and body weights for each age class are higher for the northern deer, followed by deer from the central region, with the southern deer having the lowest average.

If you don't live in an area with a lot of agriculture, food plots are a great tool to improve the quality of a deer herd. If you do live in an intensive agricultural area, timing of crop harvest and the variety of plants grown in food plots can significantly improve your success at selecting productive stand locations. Now that we have discussed the benefits of food plots, let's talk plant types.

LEARNING THE MENU

Just like there is no one vehicle that suits everyone's needs or one hunting tool that meets every hunting condition, there is no one magic plant or type of plant for the best food plots. Instead, the best food plots will contain a variety of plant types to meet the varying nutritional needs of the deer herd during the entire year.

Food plot crops can be divided into two general categories: annuals and perennials. Annuals are species that must be replanted each year, while perennials are species that will survive for several years with some ongoing maintenance and care. Annuals and perennials each have their strengths and weaknesses. Let's discuss annuals first.

This photo shows a test plot for one of the New Zealand seed varieties planted in South Carolina. Notice that on the inside of the cage the forage is 10 inches high. On the outside, deer have browsed it down to about three inches.

Annuals are popular because they are generally less expensive, on an initial planted-acre basis, than many types of perennial seeds. In addition, there are a number of good annual plant species for both warm- and cold-season plantings. With annuals you can create two-season (warm and cool) food plots by planting a mix of species. Mixes of annuals that work well include warm-season legumes such as Aeschynomene, Alyce clover, or climbing peas planted with milo. The milo provides support and cover that benefits these warm-season species. Deer will feed on the milo grain heads after the warm-season legumes have been consumed or killed by frost.

Similarly, planting a warm-season annual and then drilling a cool-season variety directly into the warm-season crop can create a two-season food plot. This technique minimizes soil preparation and utilizes any residual lime and fertilizer not used by the warm-season annual. To ensure a good stand of the cool-season crop, it might be necessary to mow the warm-season annual if too much vegetation is still available when it is time to plant the cool-season variety. A common combination of crops used to develop a two-season annual food plot is wheat top-drilled over beans or peas.

For proper deer herd management, it is critical to provide nutrition to the deer herd during summer, as well as fall and winter. In summer, bucks require nutritious forage for antler development; does need it to produce the milk necessary for maximum fawn growth before the winter stress period begins. Summer food plots also help to keep deer in the immediate area throughout the year. For that reason, annuals are critical for the warm-season planting.

■■■

"It is critical to provide nutrition to the deer herd during summer as well as fall and winter."

■■■

Annuals are also popular for the cool-season planting. In the past, nutrition has not been a primary objective of fall annuals. Rather, cool-season annuals have traditionally been planted to attract deer to open areas for observation or harvest. Small grain crops such as wheat, oats and rye are commonly used to establish cool-season annual food plots. Although these species provide a source of energy-rich carbohydrates, they are usually low in protein and mineral content.

Perennials are plant species that will survive for several years once they become established. For optimum growth and lifespan, the soil fertility must be maintained by applying lime and fertilizer once or twice annually. In addition, depending on the browse pressure and weed competition, other forms of maintenance such as mowing might be necessary.

One advantage of perennials is that they only require seedbed preparation and planting every three to five years. Hence, it is usually less expensive over a three-year period to maintain a perennial versus an annual food plot, even though the initial seed costs might be more expensive. A disadvantage of perennials is that they rarely provide forage throughout the entire year. To solve this problem, top-drill a cool-season annual like wheat into an existing perennial such as clover. Annuals that are heavy seed producers might reseed if they are mowed, lightly disked or burned. However, to ensure a good stand, annuals should be planted yearly rather than be allowed to reseed on their own.

There are more than 60 plant species traditionally planted for deer. The exact variety best for your property depends on the climate, soil and deer density.

■ ■ ■

"One advantage of perennials is they only require seedbed preparation and planting every three to five years."

■ ■ ■

FOREIGN CUISINE

In the United States there have been some blends of clovers, like those from Whitetail Institute, designed to cover a broad spectrum of growing conditions similar to those found with food plot establishment. However, many American seed companies do not consider growing forage for deer a worthy market.

In New Zealand, though, deer forage research is very serious business. The roots of this business go back to the early 1900s when several species of deer including elk, fallow deer, sika deer and even whitetails were stocked in New Zealand for sport hunting. Before then, there were no deer native to New Zealand. Without predators, these stocked herds quickly expanded and had negative impacts on the native plant communities. The New Zealand government then initiated several programs to reduce the rapidly expanding herds. One of the programs allowed farmers to trap these non-native species and use them as breeding stock for velvet antler and venison production farms.

During the last decade, these farms have become sophisticated. Currently, velvet antlers and venison are leading exports from New Zealand. As the demand for these products increased in the European and Asian markets, New Zealand began to seriously research forage varieties that maximize antler and venison production.

The forage varieties that the researchers in New Zealand developed were created specifically to provide the protein and minerals necessary to allow for maximum antler development and weight gain. Their research included the standard germination and yield tests. Then they followed through with detailed palatability and animal performance tests. These tests use antler development, weight gain and fawn production as performance indicators.

Local farmers and agricultural offices can help you choose seed blends that will flourish in a given soil type.

For example, one of the varieties the deer farmers were pleased with was an annual forage crop. The seed company in New Zealand that developed it had originally bred more than 20 varieties of this plant, each having slightly different characteristics. The varieties that germinated well and produced enough tonnage per acre were then all planted in small test plots within one fenced pasture. Animals were released in the pasture and observed to determine the top four preferred varieties. The next year, these four varieties were planted in separate pastures, and the animals' growth performance for each pasture compared. This research ensures plant forage varieties that will grow well, are palatable, and that targeted species will perform well. I am unfamiliar with any research this intensive in the U.S.

I received and tested some of these New Zealand seed varieties to determine if they would grow well in the various soils and climates in the United States. They were planted on my clients' properties in Alabama, Arkansas, Mississippi, North Carolina, Pennsylvania and South Carolina. They germinated, grew and were consumed by deer at all these locations. I collected samples at the South Carolina and Arkansas sites and had forage analysis tests performed at Clemson University. The crude protein from the Arkansas and South Carolina samples was 30.1 percent and 38.8 percent, respectively. The mineral levels were also high. It's easy to understand why the antler development and weight gain of the deer in New Zealand is so impressive.

Whether you're planning on planting traditional food plot crop varieties or trying some of the New Zealand forage varieties, food plots will help your local deer herd.

Dealing with Does

LARRY WEISHUHN

When whitetail populations exceed the carrying capacity of the land, habitat degrades and large die-offs can occur during adverse weather conditions. Doe harvests are an essential component in maintaining quality habitat, deer herds and other wildlife populations.

Tongues of wild campfire flames lashed out into the dark November sky. The tongues of the hunters around the campfire were doing a fair amount of blazing as well. Half of the hunters around the fire pit were adamantly opposed to shooting does, while the other half was strongly in favor of doe harvests.

Such arguments have been going on for many years. I well remember when the first doe hunting was allowed in Texas. Those who took does were ostracized by fellow hunters. And there were not many who did. The first year that doe hunting was allowed in the South Texas Brush Country, less than 50 does were taken, and all but about 10 of those were taken on one ranch. A lot of deer management practices have changed since then.

Today, nearly as many does as bucks are taken each year, and on some of the more intensively managed areas, there are considerably more does taken than bucks. Getting there was far from easy, and it certainly did not happen overnight.

During the early and mid-1900s wildlife departments protected does as deer populations recovered from habitat loss and, in some instances, market hunting. In essence, wildlife management personnel did such an excellent job of promoting the protection of does that it has taken years to try to convince hunters that taking does is not only okay but also necessary.

Today's hunters have embraced doe hunting across North America. Although it is difficult to compare modern doe hunting efforts from year to year and state to state, it has become abundantly clear that populations are finally being brought closer to goals across the country. For example, in the Midwest, statewide antlerless harvests increased by an average of 80 percent in a six-year span ending in 2007.

THE KEY: HABITAT

Throughout much of the white-tailed deer's range, populations have reached a point where they are beginning to damage their habitat. Unfortunately, when the habitat is adversely affected, it takes an extremely long time to recover. While whitetail populations can rebound very quickly, it takes wildlife habitat much longer. Habitat is in a constant state of change. It can be affected by changes in local weather conditions, especially in terms of a lack of rainfall, late freezes and other unseasonable weather changes. It can also be altered by changes in livestock grazing rates and practices, forestry and agricultural practices, and by the loss of adjoining habitat being converted into housing developments, shopping centers, golf courses and other uses that some humans consider important.

Of the 42 states with huntable whitetail populations, nearly every one has made a concerted effort in the past 10 years to encourage hunters to shoot more does. Increasing statewide doe harvests and season bag limits for hunters has paid off in reduced deer herds and more manageable local deer densities. Some states have accomplished these goals simply by providing bonus tags and additional doe-only seasons. Others have implemented the so-called "earn-a-buck" rule, which requires each hunter to harvest and register an antlerless deer before getting the chance to hunt for a buck. Other state agencies have used state funds to foot the bill for, or at least help offset, venison processing costs for hunters who donate deer to food pantries and Hunters for the Hungry programs.

In other instances hunters are balking because they like to see a lot of deer whenever they hunt — even if such a situation is not what is best for deer or the habitat. This seems to be especially true in the North and Southeast areas of whitetail range.

If some hunters want to see more deer, then why should we be harvesting does each year? The answer is fairly simple. The primary reason for harvesting does is to prevent overpopulation problems and the resulting habitat abuse. When overpopulation occurs, the habitat is destroyed and the entire deer population suffers, as do other animals.

Bucks and does are born at a ratio of approximately 50–50. Admittedly, there is a higher mortality rate in young males than there is in females. But if bucks and does are born at a 50–50

ratio it only makes sense to harvest them at approximately the same rate or at least one that comes close.

What happens when only bucks are harvested? The buck-to-doe ratio begins to widen, and the deer population increases because of the great number of breeding females. Soon there is an overpopulation problem, and the deer are stressed because there is not sufficient food to keep the herd healthy. The next step is habitat degradation. From there, the average size of the deer in the area begins to decrease because there isn't sufficient nutrition to develop the bodies and antlers that they have the genetic potential to grow as healthy adults.

A CASE IN POINT

A prime example of this situation was seen in the deer that live in the Texas Hill Country. Before overpopulation problems, it was not uncommon to see bucks that weighed nearly 200 pounds with massive, wide and multi-pointed racks. As the deer population increased and the amount of available food decreased, so did the average size of the deer.

During these lean and hungry years, it was not uncommon for a mature five-year-old buck to have less than six points and weigh no more than 70 pounds live weight. Does were even smaller. The population continued to increase, until during the late 1960s and early 1970s when severe deer die-offs occurred.

Today, thankfully, much has changed and the region's landowners and hunters are harvesting as many does as bucks. They're also conducting habitat and range improvements. As a result, the deer herd is again healthy, and the body and antler

Stable fawn recruitment rates of better than one fawn per doe will assure a balanced adult buck-to-doe ratio regardless of what type of management strategy is used on a property.

size of the average deer has greatly increased. However, imagine what could have happened had hunting practices not changed.

Now throw in adverse weather like a severe winter or prolonged drought. Thousands of deer can die as a result. The first to die are the older deer and the fawns, both of which are extremely important to the overall herd.

When there is insufficient forage or food to keep the deer healthy, they are more quickly and more adversely affected by diseases and parasites. In many areas of its range the whitetail's biggest disease problem is commonly referred to as "hollowbellyitis." They simply do not get enough quality food.

Thus, the next logical question we should ask, "Do we really need a lot of does to produce fawns and future bucks?"

Several years ago, while working for the state of Texas as a biologist, I established and initiated a deer management program on a 3,000-acre ranch. After doing a survey, I recommended that a total of 100 does be removed. At the time of the survey the fawn survival rate was approximately 25 percent (expressed in terms of the number of fawns reared divided by the total number of does). The deer density on the property prior to the hunting season approached a deer per every eight acres.

■■■

"A prime example of this situation was seen in the deer that live in the Texas Hill Country. Before overpopulation problems, it was not uncommon to see bucks that weighed nearly 200 pounds with massive, wide and multi-pointed racks. As the deer population increased and the amount of available food decreased, so did the average size of the deer."

■■■

After the hunters on the property harvested the recommended 100 does, they figured that would probably be all the does they'd have to harvest for a long, long time. The following year when we conducted the deer survey, there were more deer on the property than the year before. But many of the deer were fawns. After shooting the 100 does, the ranch actually had more fawns than it did the year before. Because of the significant doe harvest, the fawn survival rate increased from 25 percent (four does to rear one fawn to weaning age) to 120 percent (1.2 fawns per doe). Thus, by removing "surplus" does, the remaining does reared many more fawns to weaning age.

Essentially, by shooting does, the hunting group added a considerable number of buck fawns to the population. The following year the property was loaded with yearling bucks. That

Hunters are beginning to realize that utilizing doe tags is critical in many regions of the U.S.

year the hunters harvested 75 does. In the years that followed they took as many bucks as they did does, including a high percentage of mature bucks.

HARVEST DOES FOR BIGGER BUCKS

We had similar results using the same approach on many other operations as well. Does that are healthy and on a good year-round diet tend to produce healthy fawns. If those fawns are bucks, they will develop impressive antlers, provided they are given the opportunity to mature to three years old and older in the presence of good nutrition.

Any deer harvest scheme should include some doe harvest. The number of does harvested annually should depend on current population and target population densities, current and goal buck-to-doe ratios, fawn survival rates and habitat conditions.

In certain situations, however, the key to producing a healthy deer herd might not mean killing a lot of does. What might be required is increasing the quality and amount of food available on a sustained basis. This is normally the case in what might be considered marginal deer range. We have seen white-tailed deer continue to increase their range. Several of the prairie and midwestern states had few whitetails within their boundaries until farmers started planting crops such as soybeans, corn and various other cereal grains. These fields, which had formerly been open grassland or stands of mature forests where there was little deer forage available, greatly increased the deer's sustained food supplies. So populations flourished.

We can take a lesson from these farmers. By increasing the food supply and its quality, we can increase the number of deer that live in an area. Consider planting food plots to provide deer food throughout the year. But even in these situations, the deer herd will reach a point when it will become necessary to harvest does.

If you are not already participating in harvesting does, perhaps it is time to start. Taking does is an essential part of managing any deer herd . . . and it can also get you closer to the buck of your dreams.

In Pursuit of the Trophy Doe

TOM CARPENTER

I shoot does.

Yes, I admit it. In fact, I'm proud of the trophy does I've hunted and taken with rifle, shotgun, muzzleloader and bow. Antlerless deer fill my hunting memories. And I expect to shoot some more does before I find out what Opening Day is like in that other happy hunting ground.

Bucks are okay too. Like any red-blooded, All-American hunter, I like some antlers for the wall now and again. But where legal and when I hold the proper tag, and when my pounding heart tells me it's time to shoot a deer, I will take a doe. My hands sweat, blood races, head pounds, arms shake, breathing comes hard . . . you'd think I had a real trophy walking into my sights.

I do.

But how often have you heard, or maybe even said, one of these phrases: "Yeah, I got one. Just a doe." Or, "I settled for a doe." Or, "I could have had a bunch of does." Or, "I'm waiting until the last day."

There are two themes here. One: A doe is a second-class animal. Two: You've had only a half-success by taking an antlerless deer. Plenty of us will shoot does but make apologies for it.

She's older and smarter than the buck you shot last year, but there are no antlers. Is she a trophy?

How did these attitudes evolve? Are we saddled with them forever? Can you really feel good about shooting an antlerless deer, or are you going to make it a non-event? Let's explore.

ATTITUDES ABOUT DOES

The idea that a doe is not as good as a buck has several origins.

We have an abundance of whitetails today. Just look at harvest statistics for the state(s) you hunt. But with that wealth of deer comes complacency — the notion that deer are a commodity and that a doe is commonplace and not special.

I'm also bothered by the idea that a doe is not challenging to hunt, the macho belief that even a yearling buck is better because there's some bone growing from its head. The source of this attitude surely stems from the days when shooting does was taboo on the thin herds. Old beliefs die hard, if at all.

I remember my very first deer, a doe of course, so long ago.

Deer herds were re-building then. While every hunter in the woods didn't get an antlerless tag, you could apply as a party. An ambitious 15-year old, I coordinated the application for our family group of four, got the tag (called a party permit in those days), and was rewarded as the designated doe shooter.

I couldn't have been more excited. Any deer was fair game! You can remember what it was like to be 15.

With several seasons under my belt, I was ready for success. I picked out an opening morning stand in an old, brushy pasture on the top edge of a big riverside timber. Deer trails wound their way up from riverbottom cornfields, and I was sure deer would come through either naturally or while evading hunters below.

On stand an hour before dawn, I waited like a statue. At shooting light, the sky pink with a cloud bank rolling in, two deer trotted silently through, cautious and on a hair trigger.

The lead doe, circling to get the slight breeze in her favor, hit an opening and stopped at 50 yards. Fire flew from my shotgun and she wheeled.

I went over and found hair. Lots of it. And figured I'd only grazed her. So I went back to my post against a dead elm and thought. Then I went back, worked slowly in the direction she had fled, and within 30 yards saw a snow-white belly just across a fence, in the frozen alfalfa field. The sun wasn't even up.

She was a big deer, and she looked even bigger on the sprawling trunk of our late-60's-vintage Impala at the old country tavern where we waited to have her registered (still a rite of every successful hunt in my native Wisconsin).

There's no denying the sleek beauty of a healthy white-tailed doe. To honor the harvest of such a magnificent animal is essential.

Two hunters walked up interestedly to look at the big deer. "Hmph. Baldy," one sneered as they turned away. I deflated.

My brother Chuck was quick to point out, in a voice that could be heard as they walked away, "She's a good deer, Tom, 3-1/2, 4-1/2 years old. You think that forkhorn over there (the one laying in the bed of their fancy truck) was smarter?"

Take it from an old doe shooter. Feelings haven't changed much, and there are a lot more deer around today.

But I'm still shooting does. I still get excited when an antlerless permit arrives, just like that 15-year-old who rushed home from school every day to paw through the mail and see if the doe tag had come. I still get excited to have an antlerless tag in my pocket on opening morning. Yes, I'll shoot a doe on opening morning.

And I've never quit believing that a doe — any antlerless deer for that matter — is a trophy.

THE DOE CHALLENGE

If you still believe does are inferior deer, you're saying well, this guy just can't hunt up a buck. I can. I'm proud of those bucks, and what it took to successfully hunt them. But I'm just as excited if I get a doe, and just as proud.

And in many cases, especially if you're hunting fair-and-square, that doe is as challenging to bag as any buck.

On another hill-country farm I have hunted since childhood, there is a steep draw behind the barnyard. Cattle used to pasture there, but now it is overgrown with raspberry brambles, wild plum, some birch among the oaks, and assorted brush so thick you can't believe it. Pressured deer gravitate here. We call it The Nursery because of the rusted old swing set and tractor-tire sandbox that the land has re-claimed.

We work this out-of-the-way nook when deer become scarce elsewhere. We often see deer here. We usually get outsmarted. No matter how much thinking and second-guessing is done on how to push the cover and where to stand, the deer — usually does — go where you don't expect.

With just me and my father hunting, there were plenty of routes for deer to escape unscathed. But one season my friend Ron came to hunt. So did my brother Larry. With extra standers to post, I thought, "We've got those Nursery deer now!"

One pusher is all you need. We worked the patch three times in two days, and the deer, all does, evaded us every time.

We have shot one deer here while doing a push. I was sneaking through after a light snow and it just stood up 20 yards away, looking at me. I shot and it slumped back into its bed — a 6-point buck. The does never let that happen to them.

No whitetail is a pushover, especially a mature doe. She will use every bit of terrain and cover to her advantage.

Picking Out Adult Deer

While a good deer biologist will tell you that an antlerless harvest should consist of deer of all ages and sizes — yes, even fawns — it is understandable that you might want to be sure you're shooting an adult doe. Here are a few tricks of the doe-shooting trade that I've learned over years, to help you increase that likelihood:

- Only shoot an antlerless deer traveling with other deer, so you can compare and pick out the larger, adult deer. If you shoot a lone antlerless deer, be prepared for what you get.
- Look at the face and nose; they will be long on an adult doe. Fawns' snouts are short.
- Focus on the lead deer. An adult doe will usually lead a group of deer, especially in a firearms season when some hunting pressure is on.
- Evaluate and compare body thickness. A fawn might be as tall as its mother, but it won't be as heavy. Wait for a view that indicates which deer is widest across the shoulders, back and rump; there are differences.
- Look at tails. An adult doe's will be much longer than any juvenile's.

If you're afraid of shooting a small deer, wait until you can make a comparison.

Any deer is a good deer. But if size matters to you, refrain from shooting a lone antlerless deer.

You can't tell me these farmland does — any does for that matter — are not smart, are not hard to hunt. Rather, they are every bit as savvy as the bucks. Often more so. Who do you think teaches little bucks how to survive, how to evade hunters?

FEELING GOOD ABOUT A REAL TROPHY

If I'm making you feel better about taking a doe — that you are a good hunter, that a doe or any other antlerless deer is a good and worthy deer and deserves a spot on the meatpole — then I'm doing my job.

I like going hunting and knowing that trophies abound. I like knowing that I won't have to be disappointed by how many tines, or inches of antler, a buck possesses . . . if I'm good enough or lucky enough to get a deer at all.

I don't feel macho going home empty-handed because the right buck didn't come along. I love to hunt deer. They don't just walk into my lap, and it is a privilege to hunt one, shoot one and remember it all. No deer, not even a doe, is "easy."

We went back to that brush-choked draw, The Nursery, on the third day of the season, our motley little group of an 81-year-old dad, two middle-aged sons and a friend.

I set up my partners perfectly, two at likely escape routes and one at an oddball crossing that seemed right for the light northwest breeze. I took an angle into the cover and worked the brush slowly, carefully and methodically, like I would for cottontails. I jumped not one deer that I knew of, but upon our post-push gathering learned that no less than 6 different deer had squirted out at various points, but none in range of the standers!

West, a hundred yards over the hill, is an even tinier patch of sidehill brush called, for lack of a better name, the corner patch. I knew at least one deer had to go there, and it's a good deer hideout even if one of the six didn't escape to there across the fallow field. Everyone got into new positions and I swung way around and waded into the cover slowly.

The scene is like this.

I am in the middle of the tiny, two-acre patch of crabapple trees, old apple trees gone wild, raspberry brambles, goldenrod, tall grass and seven or eight ancient white oaks . . . a whitetail haven and heaven. Nearing a particular crabapple where deer like to hunker under the low-sweeping branches, I have to hold my shotgun above my head as I push and side-step through the thick, waist-high tangles.

A rustling arises up ahead and the shotgun lowers to my shoulder as a deer jumps from beneath the branches to begin a bound. As hooves hit the ground my brain is in automatic but full gear — the deer is now straight ahead and I know my hunting partners are out of the line of fire because I placed them — and as hooves thump again she falls to the ground, a wisp of smoke rising from my barrel and my consciousness registering what she looked like in the scope when I must have pulled the trigger.

Somebody's Shooting Antlerless Deer

These numbers, from a sampling of deer states, reveal the truth: In almost all places, antlerless animals comprise a healthy percentage of the deer harvest, sometimes the majority. If it weren't for trophy does, many of us would be going home empty-handed.

STATE	% ANTLERLESS DEER
New York	51%
Pennsylvania	49%
Georgia	68%
Texas	39%
Alabama	43%
Wisconsin	59%
Minnesota	44%
Wyoming	11%
Nebraska	36%

The quality of any hunt doesn't depend on antlers. Teamwork, time spent outdoors — and prime venison — make for the best memories.

By the time I work my way over her hooves have stopped their phantom run and she is still. I am glad for that, because she is beautiful and peaceful there in the goldenrod, stretched out in a replica of her last leap. I sit down next to her and wait.

Soon the two faster walkers arrive and we shake hands, talking quietly about our success for a few minutes. Finally Dad shuffles his way over, and with us all together I feel pretty darn good.

Every once in a while, late at night or when I just need to think of such things, I picture us out there in the Cadiz Township hills: Hunting together, hunting hard, not giving up, shooting a good deer and then gathering slowly in the sunset to admire her and then dress her out.

And I realize once again that the quest for a trophy need not be complex or difficult or expensive or have anything to do with inches of antler. Sometimes you find what you're looking for in a good deer (yes, even a doe), in hunting with people you love, and just being out there with all of it in a place that matters, with the orange sun raking low across the hills and the perfume of autumn goldenrod filling you.

Bucks in the 'Hood

WILLIAM B. GORDON

For almost 20 years the residents of Pennsylvania's Fox Chapel Borough have known that they're facing a serious ecological problem. Today they have a program in place that can serve as a model for other suburbs infested by white-tailed deer.

Fox Chapel Borough is a residential community located approximately nine miles northeast of downtown Pittsburgh. It covers almost 5,400 acres and has a population of about 5,600 residents. Most of the borough is zoned for 1-, 2- or 3-acre lots. While there are no commercial establishments in Fox Chapel,

Whitetails have proven to be the most adaptable of all big-game species with regard to human intrusion.

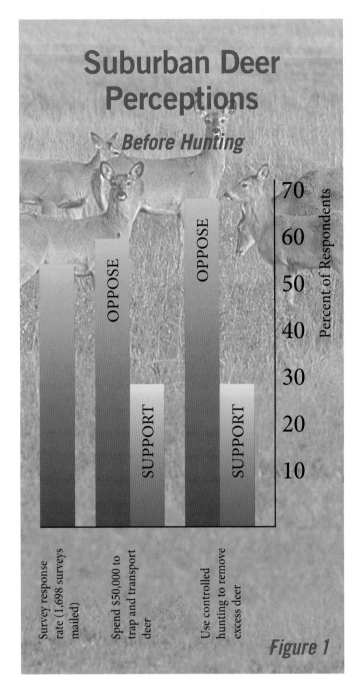

Suburban Deer Perceptions

Before Hunting

Percent of Respondents

70
60
50
40
30
20
10

OPPOSE

OPPOSE

SUPPORT

SUPPORT

Survey response rate (1,698 surveys mailed)

Spend $50,000 to trap and transport deer

Use controlled hunting to remove excess deer

Figure 1

"People who live in Fox Chapel are soon going to learn a vital lesson in wildlife ecology the hard way. Almost before the residents of this semi-rural area realize what is happening, much of the enchantment of living there may be gone. The very things which drew these people to Fox Chapel in the first place — the woodlands, the scenic beauty and the privilege of living close to nature — are being insidiously destroyed by a mammalian monster commonly called the white-tailed deer."

The council concluded that some form of hunting was the only viable alternative for reducing the size of the herd. But this concept was not well received by residents, and no management plan was enacted at that time. Concerns later resurfaced among residents. This led the council to conduct a survey of residents to determine public opinion. As you can see in Figure 1, the majority of residents were still opposed to any program to trim the deer herd.

■■■

"Some form of hunting was the only viable alternative for reducing the size of the herd. But this concept was not well received by residents."

■■■

Deer management questions were again raised five years later. Representatives of the Pennsylvania Game Commission (PGC) addressed the council at its July meeting and recommended that the borough develop a strategic management plan for reducing the size of the herd. This prompted the creation of the Wildlife Management Committee.

In September of the next year, another survey was sent to 1,768 households. This time the response rate increased to 60 percent. Of those who responded, 49 percent indicated that they could support a program to trap the deer and release them somewhere else, 64 percent could support trapping and killing the deer and giving the meat to food kitchens for the hungry, 51 percent supported conventional hunting with bow and arrow and 41 percent supported hunting with shotgun.

In December of that year, the draft Deer Management Plan was forwarded to the council, adopted and sent to the PGC for approval. The purpose of the plan was to set criteria for determining whether a deer management plan was warranted and, if so, the methods of population control.

NEED

The plan suggested that a deer management program might be instituted whenever one or more of the following conditions exist:

two golf courses, a racquet club, four churches, one private school and one wildlife reserve are located within its borders. Of the 5,400 acres comprising the borough, 365 acres are designated as parkland. Most of the land owned by the borough is heavily wooded, and one area, the Trillium Trail, is renowned for the blanket of white trillium that carpets the hillsides every spring. At least it used to.

Complaints about deer problems in Fox Chapel are nothing new. Records indicate that as far back as two decades ago residents had complained to the borough council about damage caused by deer. This prompted Roger Latham, then outdoors editor of *The Pittsburgh Press*, to write an extremely prophetic article.

1) Human health or life is in danger or expected to be in danger.
2) The health of the deer herd is adversely impacted by the lack of sufficient natural food.
3 Significant damage to the natural plant life caused by deer browsing or rubbing of antlers. (Damage to ornamental residential plantings alone was not proposed as a reason for establishing a management program.)
4) A majority of borough residents express a desire to control the size of the deer herd.

Criterion 1:

Danger to Human Health or Life

Police reports indicate that there were 45 deer killed by motor vehicles between June and November of just one year. In addition, respondents to the survey had reported 368 accidents involving deer, although no time period was specified. This high number of accidents and the potential for serious injury or death as a result was judged sufficient to warrant deer management.

Criterion 2:

Health of the Deer Herd

Based on observations of the physical condition of individual deer and the fact that many does gave birth to twins, the committee concluded that the health of the herd was good.

Criterion 3:

Damage to Natural Plant Life

White-tailed deer are known to eat almost any plant species. However, certain plants are preferred. Based on observations of browse damage to various plant types, biologists can draw some conclusions about the deer population. If highly-preferred plants are abundant, the deer population is probably lower than the carrying capacity of the land. If undesirable plants are being eaten, this generally indicates overpopulation.

Since many of the preferred browse species are prolific seed producers, the loss of these plants also negatively impacts seed-eating birds. In the longer view, the inability of certain plants to reproduce results in a decline in overall ecological diversity.

While detailed studies are sometimes required to evaluate damage caused by deer, such was not the case in Fox Chapel. Trillium Trail used to attract hundreds of visitors each spring. But the area became virtually devoid of any blossoms due to browsing by deer. Additional observations in other wooded areas showed an absence of the understory needed to sustain the forest when mature trees die. Clearly, the third criterion had been met.

Criterion 4:

Residents' Opinions

As previously indicated, the second survey showed a majority of respondents favoring one or more forms of deer management.

MANAGEMENT

If it is determined that a deer management program is warranted based on the above criteria, the plan recommends that it include one or more of the following components: herd survey, feeding restrictions, trapping, sterilization/contraception and hunting.

Herd Survey

In order to implement a management program, a desired herd size or percent reduction had to be established. As a result, it was first necessary to determine the size of the existing herd.

This was done at night by low-flying aircraft using heat-sensitive infrared videotaping. Infrared counts in the borough established an accurate count of the deer and identified areas where densities were highest.

The borough also retained the services of Dr. Ernie Wiggers, a biologist at the University of Missouri specializing in white-tailed deer. Based on his report, the data provided by the aerial survey and the available woodland habitat, the deer density the spring after the survey was at least 91 deer per square mile of habitat. That was more than 7.5 times greater than the maximum density of 12 deer per square mile recommended by forestry experts and the PGC.

Suburban Deer Perceptions

After Hunting

	NUMBER	PERCENT
Respondents who think the borough should further reduce the deer herd	1,159	87
Respondents who support the program to qualify bowhunters and match them to residents	1,030	78
Respondents who think the borough should use deer control agents	992	76

Figure 2

Feeding Restrictions

The plan concluded that supplemental feeding should be prohibited since it encourages additional population growth. In addition, it makes deer dependent on humans, promotes the spread of disease and increases the adverse impact of the deer in a localized area. The committee recommended an ordinance declaring supplemental feeding of deer illegal.

Trapping

This option includes the use of traps and/or immobilization to capture deer. However, trap-and-transfer efforts have generally proven to be labor-intensive and expensive. Aside from the problems of costs and logistics, large-scale trap-and-transfer programs require release sites capable of absorbing large numbers of relocated deer. According to the PGC, such areas are lacking in Pennsylvania.

Deer are susceptible to traumatic injury during handling, and trauma losses average approximately four percent. Capture myopathy, a stress-related disease that results in delayed mortality of captured deer, is thought to be an important and often-overlooked mortality factor. Delayed mortality rates as high as 25 percent have been reported. Thus, the council concluded that trap-and-release was not feasible.

Sterilization/Contraception

The use of fertility control agents (synthetic progestins and estrogen), once considered a viable method to solve the problem of deer overpopulation, does not appear to be a viable alternative for controlling free-ranging deer at the present time.

And before they could be used on deer that might enter the food chain, contraceptives must receive the approval of both the FDA and the PGC.

HUNTING

Hunting is recognized as an effective deer population management tool and has, in fact, been shown to be the most efficient and least expensive technique for removing deer. However, the location of homes, roads and other facilities in the borough significantly limits the amount of land available for hunting.

Therefore, the plan concluded that an alternative to conventional hunting was required and proposed the use of "deer control agents" to use rifles to shoot deer at night over baited sites. Any deer that were shot would be processed and distributed to food kitchens for the hungry.

This, then, was the deer management plan as originally submitted to the PGC. Negotiations with the PGC over the use of deer control agents continued. Finally, the commission agreed that it would allow the borough to use such agents, but only if bowhunting was also allowed to the maximum extent possible. The PGC also advised the borough council that, based on recent court decisions, no municipality in Pennsylvania has any authority to prohibit hunting. That means that any property owner can allow any licensed hunter to hunt on his or her property in accordance with all applicable game laws.

The council concluded that since it is powerless to prevent hunting, the next best thing to do to promote the safety of residents would be to set up a program to qualify bowhunters and match them to property owners who want a hunter on their property and who have land suitable for hunting. This allows the borough to check the qualifications of each potential hunter. Candidates for the program are required to complete a detailed application and, among other things, agree to only use bow and arrow, to hunt only from treestands, to shoot a doe before shooting a buck and to remove any deer from the borough before field-dressing it. The police department then conducts a background check and tests the applicant's proficiency with a bow and arrow.

■ ■ ■

"As the size of the deer herds in suburbia continues to increase due to the lack of natural predators or limited conventional hunting, their numbers can quickly exceed the biological carrying capacity of their habitat."

■ ■ ■

Once the council's decision to qualify bowhunters was published, animal activists protested. While those who demonstrated comprised a very small minority of residents, the impact on the community was divisive. The activists also filed suit in Common Pleas Court in an attempt to halt the hunting, but this action was denied.

During the first hunting season, there were no incidents of any person or animals other than deer being shot or shot at. Furthermore, because each bowhunter qualified through the police department was issued unique identifying labels for his or her arrows, we also know that there were no deer shot by qualified hunters that were not recovered.

During the 12 months following the aerial survey, 84 deer had been killed by automobiles, 79 were removed by bowhunters qualified by the police department, and at least 49 deer were removed by bowhunters who had not been qualified but were hunting legally with the permission of the landowner.

A second aerial survey was completed the next spring. The data indicated that the deer herd numbered at least 307 — a density of 103 deer per square mile of woodland and an increase of more than 12 percent from the previous year. Undoubtedly, the size of the herd increased even further during the birthing season. However, bowhunters were extremely successful that fall, taking 185 deer. Fox Chapel's deer population continues to slowly be brought back within the land's carrying capacity.

Deer in town translate into deer causing problems for residents. Fox Chapel came up with an effective management plan.

Another public survey was conducted in conjunction with a public hearing. The survey was mailed to 1,837 households, of which 1,325 responded (72 percent). As shown in Figure 2, an overwhelming majority of respondents came to support the borough's management program.

CONCLUSIONS

As the size of the deer herds in suburbia continues to increase due to the lack of natural predators or limited conventional hunting, their numbers can quickly exceed the biological carrying capacity of their habitat.

The Fox Chapel experience is convincing evidence that effective suburban deer management programs can and should include hunting.

It's a simple fact: Deer are creatures of the edge, and lush suburbia provides some of the best edge habitat in North America. However, these problems bring opportunities — namely bowhunting options for those who are willing to help educate their communities on the sport's redeeming qualities.

■■■

"Candidates for the program are required to complete a detailed application and, among other things, agree to only use bow and arrow, to hunt only from treestands, to shoot a doe before shooting a buck and remove any deer from the borough before field-dressing it."

■■■

City's Edge Whitetails

GLENN SAPIR

A s you head north along the Great White Way, theater marquees trimmed with hundreds of lights brighten the crowded sidewalks that line Broadway. Uptown, the theaters give way to chic boutiques and upscale restaurants and bars. The crowds are thinner, but are crowds nonetheless. Eventually, you leave Manhattan and enter the Bronx, where the apartment buildings stand taller. Not far from Broadway, to the east, is Yankee Stadium, perhaps the biggest single parcel of grass in the immediate area.

If you head even farther north, you'll eventually leave New York City, but it will be hard to tell from the landscape. Buildings, maybe not as tall nor as numerous, still reach to the sky, and gray asphalt still lines the sidewalks. Were it not for the infield of Yonkers Raceway or some county parks, large patches of green would be rare.

When you leave the Bronx, you indiscernibly enter Westchester County. It is an area that is contained by the Hudson River to its west, the Long Island Sound to the east. Its northern border is suburban/semi-rural Putnam County and to its northeast, the affluent suburb of Fairfield County, Connecticut.

In the county's 450 square miles are cities, towns and villages. Some of New York State's poorest citizens live in run-down tenements here; some of the nation's wealthiest dwell on several-acre estates. Rich or poor, nearly 1 million people call Westchester County home. This setting doesn't sound like a hunter's paradise. However, Westchester County has consistently produced outstanding trophy white-tailed bucks to the bow—the only legal big-game hunting tool here. It has also been the laboratory for an experimental deer management program that many sportsmen, game managers and landowners are applauding.

"With the way human populations are growing across the nation," observes NAHC Member Mike Chirico, "I think more and more areas are going to adopt the program we have initi-

■■■

"Westchester County has consistently produced outstanding trophy white-tailed bucks to the bow—the only legal big-game hunting tool here."

■■■

Westchester's deer "situation" can be perceived as a great bowhunting opportunity or . . .

ated in Westchester." Actually, game managers on Long Island and in western New York have already adopted Westchester's plan, and other states have made inquiries.

Chirico, a railroad employee and partner in Buchanan Sports, a popular retail shop for hunters in Westchester, has played an active role in shaping deer hunting regulations in his home county.

He was one of the founders of the Westchester Bowhunters Association in 1978, and served as the organization's first president. Let Chirico start tracing for you how the regulations developed.

"We formed the Westchester Bowhunters Association in 1978 to protect and improve our sport in Westchester County. In a year we had 250 members! By working hand-in-hand with the New York State Department of Environmental Conservation (DEC); Glenn Cole, wildlife manager; Steve Cook, conservation officer; Dick Henry, biologist; and with landowners, we have been able to accomplish a lot," Chirico says.

"First of all, back when I was a child, the bowhunting season was two months long. Then, because of hound hunters or bird hunters who thought the bowhunters' presence in the woods was a problem, they cut us back to one month — November 1 to December 1. When the Westchester Bowhunters Association was formed, we decided that was the first thing we needed to tackle. We put in a resolution, and we got back a longer season and an any deer rule," Henry says. "Hunters have to target more adult does."

In fact, at a meeting of the Westchester County Bowhunters Association, Henry illustrated the problem.

"Bucks in Westchester are servicing does as late as April," he said. "The does are going into estrus over and over again so that they will be bred. We've undertaken a study of road-killed does in the spring to evaluate when the fetuses they are carrying were conceived. The deer that are conceived later are less likely to survive the stresses of the next winter."

A six-point buck, with his antlers intact, was spotted dead along the Taconic State Parkway in a central Westchester location on March 24!

"Sure," Henry says, "their testosterone level is still up then; they're still participating in breeding activities."

The Westchester Bowhunters Association has helped do more than simply refine regulations. When the state began to compile a list of landowners who complained of deer damage, members found a place to hunt and landowners were pleased with the quiet solution to their problems. Later, when Lyme disease began its spread through Westchester County, other landowners sought the help of association members. When the Westchester Medical Center needed volunteers for its promising Lyme disease vaccine study, its leaders appealed to the Westchester Bowhunters Association.

"I spoke to the group at one of its meetings, and several volunteers signed up," says Donna McKenna, nurse practitioner and assistant to the vaccine-development program's leader.

Over the past 25 years, humans have pushed their way into deer habitat at a pace never before seen in the history of North America. With urban sprawl here to stay, we have come to a crossroads in deer management. How do we maintain our desire for modern landscapes while, at the same time, controlling burgeoning deer herds? The answer is simple: well-organized bowhunts. More than a decade has passed since the first sportsmen's group spearheaded efforts to do something about its community's deer herd. In the years that have passed, hundreds of towns and villages have adopted similar efforts.

All thanks to well-intentioned hunters like those in Westchester County, New York.

. . . a serious problem for residents and insurance companies.

Should We Cull Undersized Bucks?

TOM CARPENTER

Buck dispersal behavior varies greatly by region, but it generally occurs regardless of the area's deer density, its amount of quality cover and/or food sources.

Despite years of debate, the question persists among white-tailed deer hunters. Shoot the spikes, tiny forks and other spindly-racked bucks, or let 'em walk?

Deer biologists and state-employed herd managers face this question constantly, even today when much of the information that we previously believed has been contradicted with scientific research.

Before deciding whether or not to shoot undersized bucks, we must ask ourselves two questions:

1. Although culling what appear to be inferior whitetails is commonly practiced on some properties, is it just an excuse hunters use to shoot more bucks?

2. Is it scientifically prudent to remove small-racked bucks from the herd?

The answers to these questions are: "probably yes" and "probably no."

The mere presence of spikes and other undersized bucks in the herd is likely more of an indicator that something is wrong with the habitat, food abundance and size of the deer population than it is an indicator of genetic inferiority.

In southern states, where deer breeding seasons stretch into January, February and even March, there is evidence that late-born buck fawns have little to no chance of growing anything more than substandard racks when they're yearlings. Florida is a prime example. With late breeding dates and inadequate soils, the Sunshine State produces a preponderance of spikes in the yearling buck herd. In northern tier states, where the breeding season is often confined to a few weeks in autumn, small antler configurations in yearling bucks are usually attributed to harsh winters, poor nutrition and high deer densities.

■■■

"Although culling what appear to be inferior whitetails is commonly practiced on some properties, is it just an excuse hunters use to shoot more bucks?"

■■■

These effects, in both the North and South, typically cannot be changed over the course of one year. In other words, it might take a runt yearling two, three or even four years before his rack shows signs of its true genetic potential. That is why most deer biologists and managers don't consider a buck "mature" until it is at least 4½ years old.

Another interesting angle on this topic is the fact that recent scientific research indicates that high genetic diversity in whitetails has been associated with higher conception rates for adult does, better fetal growth rates for fawns and higher body weights and antler sizes for bucks. Furthermore, some researchers have been studying theories that suggest trophy buck hunting might adversely affect the herd's gene pool. This phenomenon, called "high grading" by researchers, is believed to cause a reduction in a herd's genetic potential for trophy antlers. However, as with the case of culling undersized bucks, the chances that an individual property's hunting program will permanently rewrite a region's genetic code are reduced, if not eliminated altogether, when talking about free-ranging whitetails.

Therefore, the majority of hunters in North America should concern themselves more with providing deer with great cover, abundant nutrition and the chance for bucks to live to maturity (4½ -plus years). And, all things being equal, age is the key factor. At 2½ years old, a white-tailed buck will exhibit less than 50 percent of his antler potential. By age 4½, however, he will exhibit 75 percent or more of his potential. Although there are always exceptions in the whitetail world, the majority of well-

Northern Exposure

Principles of nutrition, genetics and age and their effects on antler growth are the same throughout the whitetail's range.

A primary reason northern white-tailed yearling bucks in heavily forested areas only develop spikes or undersized racks is because of a lack of proper nutrition during the all-important first year of their lives. Often this is caused by winter severity. These northern yearling bucks, like their southern counterparts, will eventually develop larger antlers if their nutrition improves. It is extremely rare for a buck that starts out as a spike to stay that way throughout his life. In fact, there have been several documented cases of spike bucks that grew Boone-and-Crockett-class antlers by the time they reached maturity (4½ years old or older).

Human intervention cannot completely cure the problems associated with undersized yearlings, but land managers can take steps to help improve the situation by reducing the antlerless deer population and increasing the quality and quantity of the daily food supply through food plots and native browse enhancements.

fed bucks in North America will grow racks gross-scoring 140+ B&C inches at maturity.

Early studies on the culling of spike bucks netted mixed results. Some studies on Texas deer showed that culling spikes was effective in helping the other bucks in the herd grow larger, probably because of a reduced deer density. However, a massive culling study in South Texas by famed biologist Dr. Mickey Hellickson concluded there was no difference in antler quality when spikes were removed from the herd. Hellickson's study was conducted over an eight-year span on a 25,000-acre property.

So, if you happen to own a large block of whitetail habitat, or hunt in an area where you can maintain some control over the harvest of particular animals — and you want to grow and hunt mature bucks — you should not cull any young bucks based solely on the justification of "removing them from the gene pool."

Perhaps the biggest reason why we should not cull young bucks centers on the complex phenomenon of deer dispersal. Numerous studies have shown that 50 to 80 percent of all young bucks are inclined to move two to 20 miles (or more) from their birth range and establish new home ranges when they are 18 to 22 months old. This dispersal behavior varies greatly

Antler Answers

Based on the research conducted in Michigan, Georgia, Texas and other states, much has been learned about antler development in white-tailed deer. Here are some of the key conclusions reached as a result of all this research:

1. Antler development is genetically based. While all white-tailed bucks have genetics to grow antlers, not all have the same genetic potential for large antlers. This potential is only realized, however, if the animal is provided adequate nutrition and is allowed to grow to maturity.

2. The old adage, "once a spike, always a spike" has been proven false by scientific research. In fact, several cases have been documented where spike bucks grew into Boone-and-Crockett-class animals when they reached maturity.

3. Regardless of whether a fawn is born early or late, it does not affect his genetic potential for antlers. However, those born late in the summer or early in the fall are normally deprived of excellent nutrition due to changes in vegetation.

4. The four factors that most affect antler growth are: age, nutrition, injuries and stress. Stress comes in many forms, including weather and dominance behavior from other bucks and maternally related does.

5. Bucks and does each provide 50 percent of a male offspring's genetic potential for antler development. While you can't see the potential a doe provides for antler development, by carrying on a program of removing inferior antlered bucks and leaving only the bigger antlered bucks to do the breeding, the genetics of does is also improved in future generations.

6. For decades it was generally believed that when a doe gave birth to twin fawns they had the

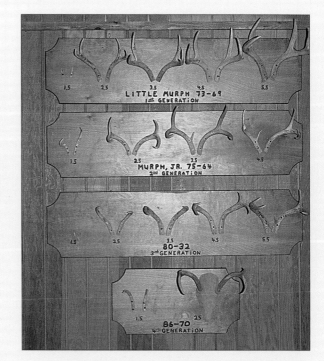

same father. Recent advancements in genetic testing has proven this to be false. One of the more comprehensive studies was conducted in Texas by Dr. Randy DeYoung. That study revealed that 22 percent of twin fawns had different fathers.

7. Periods of nutritional stress can help hunters identify the herd's best bucks. Some yearling bucks produce forked racks even in a nutritionally deprived situation. This is a sure sign that these are the bucks with the best antler potential. These are deer you definitely want to let walk so they can pass on those genes to their sons.

8. For most places in North America, age 4½ is the year when bucks display signs of their true genetic potential. However, there are some regions, including South Texas, Iowa and Wisconsin, where bucks don't hit their peak antler growing days until they are 5½ years old or older.

by region, but it generally occurs regardless of the area's deer density, its amount of quality cover and/or food sources. Many factors contribute to this behavior, including pressure from dominant bucks and, in a surprisingly greater degree, pressure from maternally related adult does. Dispersal distances can be delayed and/or decreased when buck fawns are orphaned during hunting season. However, the young bucks invariably relocate a substantial distance from their birth range.

Given these realities, what is the recipe for management success when small-antlered bucks are abundant? Enlist the help of a local deer biologist or manager and obtain ballpark estimates of your area's deer density and the land's preferred carrying capacity (PCC). For example, let's say your area is home to roughly 50 deer per square mile of habitat (pre-hunt) and the PCC is 35 deer per square mile. Given this overabundance, your first course of action should be to harvest enough does to

In the North, especially when winters are severe, the vast majority of yearling bucks might grow short spikes.

bring the density closer to goal. If the land is already providing adequate and ample nutrition, this one step — along with passing up what you previously viewed as "cull bucks" — might be all that's needed to drastically improve antler development.

It can really be that simple. However, you have to be willing to harvest antlerless deer when biologists determine that a herd has exceeded the carrying capacity of the land. As a responsible land steward, you are the ultimate deer manager, because you decide when to squeeze the trigger or release an arrow.

To achieve the best results, antlerless harvests need to be thought through from more than just a shear numbers standpoint. Just 10 years ago, many quality deer managers targeted the biggest, healthiest does for harvest. And, if herds needed large numbers of does harvested, the biggest and best mothers were routinely removed. Recent research, however, has taught us that these deer are not only the herd's best mothers, they tend to produce the largest buck fawns. These bucks, in turn, exhibited the best antler traits, on average, earlier in life than late-born buck fawns of the same age class. As a result, managers switched their efforts to targeting yearling does and doe fawns. Although the new tactic helped reduce overall deer densities, another problem arose when researchers learned that buck fawn recruitment also plummeted. The reason? For reasons not yet completely understood by researchers, healthy, mature does tend to produce nearly half as many buck fawns

as undernourished prime-age does. Some theorize that this is nature's way of self-correcting the sex ratio of the deer herd.

In short, you can't stockpile bucks on a typical deer hunting property (< 500 acres), but you can — through self restraint — lower deer densities and spare bucks from harvest in hopes that they will live to maturity and, hence, display their trophy-class potential.

Last, but certainly not least, never underestimate the need for quality food. A white-tailed buck will never reach his potential if he does not have ample forage available around the clock, year-round. If you plan on supplementing natural foods with crops, be aware that a few small "kill plots" will not cut it. A good rule of thumb is to plant at least 10 percent of your property's surface area in food plots; more is better. It is also crucial to ensure your plots are planted in adequate soils. A food plot plant is only as good as the soil in which it is grown. Poor soils will produce poor plants, which will yield little nutritional value for your deer.

Culling young bucks is a complicated issue with many prongs. Given all that we know on this subject, the short answer is to "let them walk," and switch your attention to matters you can control: age, nutrition and deer densities. With proper food, cover and reduced competition from other deer, undersized yearling and 2-year-old bucks can, in fact, produce trophy-class racks by the time they reach maturity.

CHAPTER 2

Understanding Whitetails

Anglers have scrutinized "activity" charts for decades. Figure out what time of the day the fish are most likely to feed, and you don't have to spend all day on the water staring at a motionless bobber. But can we really predict, months in advance, which days and times during the season deer are most likely to move?

Dr. Grant Woods is a deer researcher who grew up in Missouri. His story "Dark Secrets of Daytime Deer" kicks off this chapter in style. Grant's life and livelihood are tightly tied to whitetails. As hard as we hunters hunt, Grant probably accumulates more information about whitetail behavior and biology in one year than many of us will gain during a lifetime perched in treestands, still-hunting or scouting.

And Grant is not alone. Scientists across the whitetail's range have dedicated uncounted days and dollars trying to unlock whitetail mysteries. We humans are at least as curious as a big, old, foot-stomping whitetail doe.

In this information-packed chapter, you will find nuggets of knowledge that you'll do well to carry afield with you every season. None of the authors of these articles (nor the scientists who researched them) could suggest that you bank all your efforts on their findings. Instead, they'll all quickly tell you that what captivates us so about the white-tailed deer is its unpredictable nature. And in the final analysis, persistence coupled with smart hunting strategy is rewarded in the whitetail woods.

Our hope is that this chapter helps you hunt a bit "smarter" this season . . .

■ ■ ■

Dark Secrets of Daytime Deer

DR. GRANT WOODS WITH DAVE MAAS

Unless you are among the lucky few who can hunt whenever they want, planning when to hunt is as important as where to hunt. Most hunters must schedule their hunts weeks or even months in advance. They usually plan to hunt during the rut or when preferred deer food sources will be available. Although breeding dates and food source timing are important considerations, they might not be the best criteria for scheduling a hunt.

Because deer might breed and feed at night, the key is knowing when deer will be most active during daylight hours.

Hunting great sign will not compensate for nocturnal deer activity. One of my long-term research projects focused on deer behavior associated with large rubs. To ensure "real world" results, the study was conducted in an area that received heavy hunting pressure. Activity-triggered cameras were used to photograph deer near

rubs. The photos revealed that only a small percentage of the rub activity occurred during daylight hours. Nothing is more frustrating than hunting over great sign and failing to see deer.

Many hunters know that there will be a surge of deer activity just before the first strong cold front of the season. I always try to pick a stand near a preferred food source and hunt just before that initial cold front passes. However, the weather is not predictable, weeks or even days, in advance and, therefore, can seldom be used to plan a hunt.

As a result, I began trying to identify predictable factors that influence daytime deer activity. Like many researchers and writers, I initially studied the effectiveness of two moon orbit characteristics that are frequently used to predict daylight deer activity — moon phase (new, waxing, full and waning) and moon position

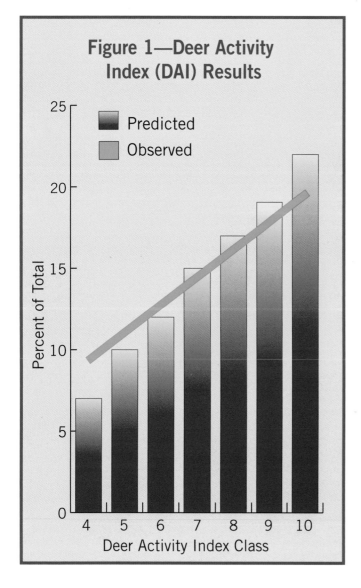

Figure 1—Deer Activity Index (DAI) Results

Predicted
Observed

Percent of Total

Deer Activity Index Class

(overhead or underfoot). These two characteristics have probably been used so often for prediction because they are easily observed by the naked eye.

Most fishermen are aware of these through the lunar tables published to predict fish feeding times. The moon's gravity pulls on large bodies of water and causes two high tides each day—one when the moon is directly overhead and the other when the moon is underfoot (on the far side of the earth). This gravitational pull on water is thought to influence fish feeding behavior.

However, this theory neglects to consider how deer differ from fish. A deer's diet is composed of plants, while most game fish are predators. Although the moon's gravitational effect on water might increase baitfish activity and trigger feeding behavior in predator fish, it does not affect when a deer's food source will be available. Scientific research results have shown that there is no relationship between daylight deer activity and moon phases.

To learn more about the moon, I began working with a national astronomical observatory, obtaining data on several additional characteristics of the moon's orbit. To my knowledge, these characteristics had not previously been compared to day-

time deer activity. Two of these characteristics are the moon's declination (angle north or south of the earth's equator) and its distance from the earth's surface. These orbit patterns change daily, but the variations cannot be seen by the naked eye.

THE RESEARCH

I started a research project on a 6,000-acre property in South Carolina that required the observation and harvest of wild, free-ranging deer (not penned). The Mt. Holly project was designed to demonstrate sound deer management strategies by balancing the adult sex ratio and allowing bucks to survive to mature age classes. Hence, the goal was to harvest several does and a limited quota of mature bucks; immature bucks were passed.

Observation and harvest data were collected predominately by wildlife biologists with a doctorate or master's degree to ensure that all necessary biological and observation data were recorded. These biologists harvested deer by using standard hunting techniques, primarily hunting from treestands, and followed all state regulations and fair chase guidelines. Stand sites were usually near seasonal food sources (primarily acorns) and travel corridors. Rattling, grunt calls, decoys and various other techniques were used. During four hunting seasons at Mt. Holly these researchers observed 2,900 wild, free-ranging deer and harvested 435.

This provided an unparalleled set of observation data to compare with moon orbit characteristics for predicting daytime deer activity. I used statistical tests to determine if the astronomical data could be used to accurately predict days with the greatest daytime deer activity. The results showed that certain moon orbit characteristics, including declination and distance between the moon and earth, could be used to accurately predict days when deer were most active. Based on the statistical analysis, I devised a formula that broke days down into seven classes of low to high deer activity.

With the formula in place, I ran an entire year's worth of spreadsheet data. This provided daily deer activity predictions. The predictions were given a numeric value of "4" (low activity) through "10" (high activity). I used these predictions to schedule the next year's hunts at Mt. Holly. South Carolina's deer season is long, and bag limits are liberal. However, the researchers had to travel 200 miles to the project site. Because most of the biologists had "real" jobs with agencies or universities, some hunts were scheduled during holidays. Unfortunately, that year many of the holiday hunts occurred on days with low deer activity predictions. To ensure we had a study of all activity predictions, we also scheduled hunts for the days with predicted high levels of deer activity.

THE RESULTS

That season, 422 hunts were required to harvest the number of deer needed for the project. A hunt was considered a full morning or afternoon; a full day of hunting equaled two hunts. During the hunts, each researcher recorded the amount of time spent hunting and the number of bucks, does, fawns and unidentified deer observed.

Moon phase might be only one small factor in lunar impacts on whitetail movement.

To ensure the data accurately reflected deer activity, it was required that a minimum of four researchers hunted at the same time from different stand locations. To determine the level of deer activity for each hunt, the total number of deer observed by the researchers was divided by the total number of minutes spent in the stand. Using an average of several hunters' observations provided a more accurate measure of deer activity than the observations of a single hunter. This reduced the effects of an individual hunter not seeing any deer because of poor stand location, poachers, predators or other events in the area.

Before any hunters went afield, I extrapolated my deer activity data and entered it into a chart based on the volume of earlier data and strength of the statistics (Figure 1). For example, I predicted deer would be almost twice as active during daylight on "9" days than on "5" days. For hunting purposes, this would mean that a hunter would have to hunt two times during "5" days to see as many deer as he would when hunting a day with a "9" ranking.

As indicated by the blue "observed" line in Figure 1, the Mt. Holly experiment proved my hypothesis true . . . for the most part. That year, the Mt. Holly research hunters observed 640 deer during 1,134 hours on stand. On average, the researchers observed 76 percent more deer on days rated "8" or higher than on days rated "6" or lower.

To test skepticism and determine that the results were not limited to South Carolina, several wildlife biologists and large hunting clubs conducted similar studies across North America. Data from these sources reflected the same trends. The Weller Mountain Hunt Club conducted one of the other larger studies in New York's Adirondack Mountains. In that study, 130 research hunters logged daily observational data from late September through early December. Although the results were not as stark as those seen at Mt. Holly, the New York hunters, while standing hunting, observed 54 percent more deer on days rated "8" or higher than on days rated "6" or lower.

WHAT ABOUT MOON PHASES?

With nearly two decades of additional studies in the books since the Mt. Holly experiment, researchers have garnered additional insights on deer activity in relation to lunar forces. For example, the deer activity index actually does seem to hinge on the "normal" timing of the hunter's moon (second full moon after the autumnal equinox), even though the index is not predicated on moon phase. The hunter's moon (also called the "rutting moon") typically falls between the end of October and the first 10 days of November. When this occurs, hunters should experience a "classic" rut, with the timing of the seeking, chasing and breeding phases being very predictable.

However, observational data from the past 15-plus years has shown discrepancies in deer activity patterns during years when the hunter's moon occurs later in the cycle (November 13, 14 or 15). This typically occurs every three years, and during those years predictions for daily deer activity become unreliable. During these years, daily deer activity is erratic, and the rut seems to progress much more rapidly than in "normal" years. In fact, studies by other researchers have indicated that when the rutting moon arrives late, the rut's seeking phase will begin three or four days before the full moon. Then, when the full moon occurs, the chasing phase will be condensed and much more intense than normal. This will then be followed by a breeding phase that kicks in within a day or two of the full moon's appearance, rather than a week after its arrival.

Some studies show that when the "hunter's moon" arrives later in November, the rut's seeking phase will begin three to four days earlier than normal.

Why the disparity? No one seems to know for sure. These contradictions in deer activity have led researchers and behaviorists to theorize that other factors play larger roles in daytime deer activity than previously thought. These activities include wind speed, hunting pressure, food availability and air temperature.

ACTIVITY ENHANCERS AND SUPPRESSORS

Lunar-based deer activity predictions cannot lead you to the best places to hunt. Hunters still need to use their knowledge of food availability, hunting pressure and habitat type to determine where to hunt. These factors vary greatly, depending on location and season.

Human pressure is perhaps the "mother of all rut suppressors," especially when daytime air temperatures rise above seasonal averages. In an ongoing lunar-based deer activity study in New York, famed deer behaviorist Charles Alsheimer has concluded that more than 55 percent of deer activity occurs during daylight in areas where there is little to no human pressure. The activity level drops to only 30 percent in areas that receive moderate to high human activity in the form of hunting, hiking and bird watching.

Air temperature, especially unseasonable highs, can nearly shut down daily deer activity altogether. In Northern environments, this means daytime temperatures above 60 degrees during early autumn and above 45 degrees during the rut. Southern deer have a somewhat higher tolerance for warm weather, but the whitetail's heavy hide and coat do not provide much in the way of ventilation. Hence, deer shut down during such spells, moving only when they have to, and limiting those movements to short jaunts between bedding and feeding areas.

Barometric pressure is also believed to play a major role in daytime deer activity. To illustrate this point, Illinois biologist Keith Thomas conducted a comprehensive study that concluded most whitetail feeding activity occurred when the barometric pressure hovered between 29.80 and 30.29, regardless of whether the pressure was rising or falling.

Food quality and availability also rank high on the lists of activity enhancers and suppressors. For example, the average percent of acorns found in the stomach content of deer harvested at Mt. Holly changed drastically from month to month and year to year. A stand in an oak flat that was productive one October (when the stomach content averaged 43 percent acorns) was probably not productive for deer sightings during the next October (when the average stomach content was only 3.2 percent acorns).

The deer herd's adult sex ratio will also dictate the amount of daytime activity a hunter sees during the rut. Areas with adult doe-to-antlered buck ratios exceeding 3:1 generally result in decreased deer sightings among hunters who hunt during the rut's seeking, chasing and breeding phases. This is primarily due to the fact that white-tailed does are less active than bucks during the rut. When a property has far more adult does than antlered bucks, bucks do not have to roam far and wide when the majority of does enter estrus. Likewise, more deer sightings are typically reported when local populations have an adult sex ratio that is 2:1 or less.

CONCLUSIONS

Although we still cannot pinpoint the exact reasons why, ongoing studies clearly indicate the moon has a distinct effect on white-tailed deer and their daily activity behavior, especially during the rut. In fact, the seasonal fluctuations in year-to-year lunar characteristics and the resulting rut activity might explain why hunters often report, "There was not much of a rut this year," or "I hunted near fresh rubs and scrapes but did not see many deer."

Therein lies the value of lunar-based deer activity predictions. Not everyone has the vacation days nor flexibility to block out a whole month for hunting rutting whitetails. The benefit of lunar research, all things being equal, is the ability to know which days and weeks offer the best odds for success. However, lunar-based deer activity charts, calendars and predictions should not be viewed as replacements for sound hunting techniques. Instead, hunters should use such information as another collective tool for getting the most out of each day spent afield.

What Whitetails See

LARRY WEISHUHN WITH LUKE HARTLE

To us humans, camo, plaid and blaze are obvious. But deer look at hunting clothing with a different eye.

What do white-tailed deer see when they encounter a hunter in the woods? Do they see merely a shape that blends in with the surroundings? Or do they see a bright form like a beacon in the night? How well can whitetails see? Better than humans? How much better? These questions have been on deer hunters' minds, really, since the first scientific study was conducted nearly 20 years ago. What we've learned has given us deeper insight into the whitetail's most underrated, and possibly debated, senses.

HOW WELL CAN DEER SEE?

The two most exhaustive scientific studies on deer vision were conducted at the University of Georgia, both under the super-vision of famed research biologist Dr. Karl Miller. In the latest study, Dr. Miller and researcher Gino D'Angelo concluded that whitetail vision is about five times better than that of a human with 20/20 vision. The study's results, published last year, indicate that what a human sees at 100 feet away appears as if it is just 20 feet away to a whitetail. The researchers, however, also concluded that whitetails do not possess the ability to focus clearly. Therefore, although they can acutely detect movement and shapes better than humans, deer seem to be somewhat farsighted.

We have also learned that deer can basically see into two color wavelengths: blue and yellow, and that deer can detect light about 1,000 times below our threshold in the blue and ultraviolet wavelengths. Furthermore, we now know that deer

Hunter movement saves more whitetails than colored clothing does.

to 270 degrees. This is far greater than the 180 degrees (140 degrees binocular) of peripheral vision in humans. A whitetail's wider peripheral range is accomplished via the size of its eyes and their spatial positioning on the sides of the head.

This perhaps partially explains why deer bob their heads when they encounter perceived threats. With the large separation between the eye sockets, there is a loss is depth perception and, hence, both eyes cannot focus on an object that's relatively close.

WHAT DO DEER REALLY SEE?

In that first study, which was first reported on at the 16th Annual Southeast Deer Study Group meeting, UG researchers Dr. Miller, Brian Murphy and Larry Marchinton, along with Gerald Jacobs of the University of California and Jay Neitz of the Medical College of Wisconsin, examined photopigments of white-tailed deer.

Quoting from the paper's abstract, "All aspects of vision depend ultimately on the absorption of light by photopigments. The retinas of white-tailed deer, like those of other ungulates, contain a mixture of rod and cone photoreceptors."

To paraphrase the research procedure, these scientists attempted to determine what deer see by using sophisticated equipment and techniques. A contact lens electrode positioned on the eye of anesthetized deer sensed light-evoked potentials.

Again to quote, "The eye was stimulated with a rapidly pulsed, monochromatic light: variations in pulse rate, stimulus wavelength and adaptation state of the eye allowed preferential access to signals from different classes of photoreceptors. Recordings were obtained from nine white-tailed deer. Three classes of photopigment were detected. One of these is the photopigment contained in rods; it has peak sensitivity of about 496 nm, a value greatly similar to that found for rod photopigments in other mammals. These measurements also reveal the presence of two classes of cone. One contains a photopigment maximally sensitive in the middle wavelengths; the other cone class has a sensitivity peak in the short wavelengths."

"In light of what is known about the relationship between photopigments and vision in other species, these results suggest two likely characteristics of cone-based (i.e., daylight) vision in deer: 1) deer should be relatively less sensitive to long wavelength lights than other mammals (i.e., humans) and 2) deer would be expected to have dichromatic color vision."

THE CONNECTION TO HUNTING

Knowing how a deer's eyes work is important to hunters because it allows us to understand how deer see us in the woods and how our clothing may or may not camouflage us from being detected. One of the most debated aspects of these research projects has been the effect of UV brighteners in camouflage, blaze-orange and other hunting garments.

According to a research report from Atsko Inc., a manufacturer of garment cleaning products, to apply what has been

do not likely see colors as we see them. To them, blues and yellows appear as various shades.

When combined with the insights learned from the first University of Georgia studies, these conclusions provide hunters with more insights into deer behavior in relation to their biological makeup.

Neither study tested the peripheral vision of deer. However, researchers and behaviorists tend to agree that the whitetail possesses a peripheral vision range somewhere between 250

learned about visual systems of deer, one must determine under what ambient light the garment is viewed.

In direct sunlight at high noon there are longer wavelengths, and we humans see no effect from UV brighteners. As the earth rotates and light conditions change toward dusk or dawn, or on days of heavy overcast skies or dark shade, the amount of UV and short blue light decreases; meanwhile "the fraction of total light contributed by UV increases greatly," according to a report by Atsko.

Humans see such effects only on white or light-colored garments. Deer, however, should be able to see these same effects on almost any color. But even with deer, the surroundings are important. The Atkso report says that natural foliage is deficient in blue and UV wavelengths. It says that other variations such as motion, pattern size, specular reflectance and brightness in long wavelengths are also important, but in the report these factors were neglected because humans are capable of observing and correcting them. That's an interesting way of discussing hunting basics.

■■■

"Good woodsmanship, slow movement and attempts by hunters to try to blend in with their background and surroundings are as important as ever to deer hunting success."

■■■

Utilizing surrounding cover to break up the human form is important no matter what you're wearing or how deer really see color.

According to Atsko, if you wash your hunting clothes in a "brighter-brights" detergent, it might contain fluorescent whitening agents. These whitening agents release energy gathered through the UV spectrum in small bands of short blue wavelengths. According to the Atsko report, "Deer are much more sensitive than humans to the shorter wavelengths of light. Deer have a blue cone that picks up light most humans cannot see. This light is perceived as bright blue in the dichromatic (two-color) eye of the deer. This light occurs on garments of any color, from camouflage to blaze orange if brighteners are present."

Deer have two cones that allow them to see blue and yellow. However, deer lack photoreceptors for seeing the differences in the colors of objects that reflect yellow-green, green, yellow, orange and red. According to Dr. Neitz, deer should be less sensitive to long-wavelength light (orange and red especially) than humans. Reportedly, under low-light conditions, deer switch to using rods (used to see black, white and shades of gray). At that point, the light supposedly perceived by deer is a bright gray. We humans see color better than deer do in poor light conditions. Deer lack the red cones we have. Therefore, if blaze orange has not had any brighteners applied, deer should not see the brightness of the orange as well as humans see it.

Whitetails, in having dichromatic color vision, are not unlike some humans who are colorblind and lack the red cones. Humans with this form of color blindness see blues as blues and the rest of the color spectrum from green to red as the color yellow. Thus, and here is where it gets interesting, deer should perceive blaze orange and most of the green/brown camouflage without brighteners as yellowish green.

Therefore, blaze orange and green/brown camouflage patterns without brighteners would blend in with the world of green and yellow leaves, green and yellowish brown grass, green trees and brown tree trunks, because all these would be seen as yellows by deer. In the case of blaze orange, fellow hunters can readily see it, but the hunter wearing it would not be seen in the same way by deer. A lack of brighteners in or on our hunting clothes or the blaze orange that we wear while afield might prevent us from being quite as visible to deer, but it is not an excuse for sloppy hunting techniques.

Now that we know how deer see, how well they see and what colors they probably can and can't see, we know that it's best to err on the side of caution when formulizing hunting strategies. What are your best bets? Wear soft clothing that blends in with your surroundings and is as UV-free as possible. Move slowly and keep the wind in your face and the sun at your back.

Treeing Your Buck

TIM JONES

Over the past decade, many hunters have tried to replace woodcraft with technology. Many of us don't know the difference between a white pine and a red pine because we no longer pay attention to such things. We don't build a fire from wood we've cut ourselves. We don't know what plants to touch and not to touch. And you can't gain all this knowledge by reading about it on the Internet.

Human nature being what it is, today's deer hunters are always looking for an easy answer. We want to know for certain that we'll absolutely get a shot at a 10-point buck by blowing a "Hunter Grunter" call on the next-to-last day of the season during a light southeasterly breeze, a waxing moon and after dousing the area with "Big Stink Rut Lure."

If only deer hunting were that easy. Instead, year in and year out it's the hunter who knows (or who pays a guide who knows) the most about deer behavior in the area being hunted, who most often takes home the prize.

■■■

"Understanding these preferred plant species where deer are likely to feed, bed, rub and scrape can stack the odds in your favor."

■■■

A big part of that equation is understanding the land we hunt — the woods, swamps and farmland fringes where the deer live. Two important features that define the world deer live in are topography (the lay of the land) and plant growth. Often the two go hand in hand, but in most deer hunting situations, plant growth is the more important of the two.

You don't have to spend much time hunting whitetails to discover that deer use the plants around them in much the same way that humans use buildings. For deer, some plant communities — trees, shrubs, forbs, grasses and crops — are the equivalent of your local supermarket, just loaded with goodies to eat. Some plant varieties at various stages of growth are like your home, creating a comfortable place to relax and ruminate. Other plants are like the local gym, providing the equipment needed to exercise vital muscles. Another plant community might function like your town's emergency Civil Defense shelter — a place to retreat in extremely severe weather or in the face of invasion. And, finally, other plants in the deer's world function like a singles bar — a place to pick up a willing member of the opposite sex. The only thing deer don't have is the equivalent of offices, factories, shops or schools — their only "job" is survival. And only quick learners live.

Since wildlife biology emerged as a science in the 1930s, a lot of studies have been done on the relationships between white-tailed deer and the plants that they need to survive. Most of these works have focused on the plants that deer eat — particularly those plants that have commercial value to humans. And many northern states have studies on winter deer yards — which are created by trees of a certain age and species growing in a specific area. And, recently, some studies of rubbing and scraping behavior are taking note of the species, size and location of the trees involved.

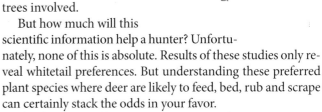

But how much will this scientific information help a hunter? Unfortunately, none of this is absolute. Results of these studies only reveal whitetail preferences. But understanding these preferred plant species where deer are likely to feed, bed, rub and scrape can certainly stack the odds in your favor.

Here's an example. Last season, my two hunting partners and I were doing some quiet "pushes" on a hillside in Vermont. My assignment was to watch a certain bench on the hillside where the deer often travel. A few days earlier, a high wind had blown over two very large trees on opposite ends of that bench — one a spruce, the other a sugar maple. Those trees represented a ready source of fresh browse at a time when snow was beginning to limit feeding opportunities. I couldn't watch them both, but I knew that deer in that area relish sugar maple and eat spruce only when they're starving.

Take the time to learn what plant species your hunt area's deer prefer to eat.

I chose a seat where I could cover the most likely route for escaping deer and where I could watch behind me — away from the push — for deer moving in on that downed sugar maple. I ignored the spruce, as I knew the deer would.

The push failed to move any deer. One of my partners had come through, and we were quietly waiting for the second, when I saw a fawn heading for the maple. Seconds later, a doe appeared. By the time the third deer showed, I had a solid rest and was watching through the bright Swarovski scope cranked up to 9X. It was easy to see the spikes, and my Vermont rifle season ended with a touch of the trigger on my Ruger .308 Win.

DO YOUR HOMEWORK

As a starting point for their study of deer and trees, hunters should take advantage of any research done locally. Contact the nearest regional office of your state's wildlife agency and ask the deer biologist about studies on deer foods, winter cover or breeding behavior. A call to any nearby university with a wildlife management program can also yield information. But if that work was done more than a few miles from your hunting area, don't expect it to yield any sure-thing clues. Still, any general knowledge you take to the field is going to help.

To better understand the nature of the problem, take a moment to consider how adaptable whitetails really are. At the northern edges of their range, they share habitat with moose, wolves and woodland caribou — creatures adapted specifically to a climate of deep snows, bitter cold and short growing sea-

sons. Thousands of miles south in Mexico, they thrive in arid, desert habitat. In between, they inhabit deep forests, farmland and suburban backyards.

In other words, the plants that are absolutely key to deer survival in one area don't even grow in others. And you don't have to travel from Minnesota to Texas to see the changes. Some years, oak trees are the key to finding deer near my home in southern New Hampshire. But where I hunt in Vermont — only a little more than 100 miles away — there's not an oak to be found.

It's been estimated that deer will feed on approximately 600 species of plants. Still, a prime food source in one area might be totally ignored in others. In one classic study in my home state, biologists cut fresh red elder, a prime browse in the northern part of the state, and fed it to a penned herd of deer a little farther south. Even with nothing else available, the deer refused to eat it for four days!

Fortunately for hunters, however, we don't need scientists to tell us what plants are important in our hunting area. The deer will give us that information if we look. All we need is enough knowledge to be able to decipher what the deer are telling us.

BASIC BIOLOGY

You might not be able to tell the difference between a hemlock and a spruce, a greenbrier and bullbrier, or a bitterbrush and willow, but the deer can! When the deer in your area show you what plant species are important to them, you can identify them by species, learn about their habitat preferences, and begin to unlock the secrets of the area you hunt.

Start with a visit to any good bookstore, especially one that specializes in nature books. A general guide such as the Golden Press *Trees of North America* will help get you started, while a regional guide to trees and shrubs, and a wildflowers guide, will let you sort out the rest. Carry these in your pack or vest while you're out hunting and scouting. When you see evidence of deer utilizing a specific plant, take a moment to note the species and location. It won't take long to see patterns emerge.

PLANT CATEGORIES

For a hunter's purposes, it helps to identify broad categories of plants that are important to deer:

Crops. If you live in a farming area, chances are that one or more of the crops in neighboring fields is helping to feed the deer. Soybeans, clover, alfalfa, corn, winter rye and a host of others are all utilized, and no hunter in farm country would think of ignoring this impact on deer behavior. Standing corn is also an often overlooked shelter for deer — they'll bed in these vast fields during summer and fall.

Forbs. For a hunter's purposes, forbs are herbaceous plants other than grasses, generally growing in open areas. In other words, weeds. Deer eat lots of 'em, and occasionally hide in 'em.

Shrubs. They're defined as low-growing multi-stemmed, woody plants. Bushes. Again, shrubs are often a key food source and are occasionally used as cover.

Trees. They serve so many functions for deer that it's best to break them down into four subcategories:

Mast-bearing hardwoods such as oaks, beeches, hickories and chestnuts are the big guns of the tree world for deer. Except for some agricultural crops, nothing draws deer like abundant mast. One of the few generalities that holds up from coast to coast is that deer generally prefer the sweet acorns from oaks in the white oak group (white oak, post oak, chinquapin, chestnut oak, and so on) to the more bitter, tannin-rich acorns of the red oak group (red oak, black oak, pin oak, willow oak, water oak, and so on). Fortunately, it's easy to tell which group the oak tree you're looking at is in — even without identifying the species. White oak leaves generally have rounded lobes, while red oaks generally have pointed lobes or at least a pointed leaf tip. You can also sample an acorn or two. The white oak acorns will taste sweet, while the red oak acorns are bitter.

A couple of other facts about most mast-bearing trees: Most white oaks produce acorns each year, while red oaks drop heavily only every other year. However, be aware that red oak acorns resist decay better than white oak acorns.

Beeches are inconsistent mast producers, but in abundant years will draw deer (and bears and turkeys) like a magnet. Beech trees are also prime scrape locations, at least in the Northeast where I do most of my hunting. I think it's because the branches swoop low to within a deer's reach and are tough enough to withstand repeated chewing and rubbing. That information helped me to see (unfortunately not shoot) the biggest buck I've ever laid eyes on.

It happened like this: I was hunting an unfamiliar area in New Brunswick, Canada, alternately rattling and moving to scout new areas. On a maple-covered hillside that showed lots of indications of deer use but no patterns, I noticed a large beech tree far up the hill. I detoured, found a huge scrape beneath the tree, and set up an ambush. The next morning a vagrant breeze betrayed me to the buck just before he stepped clear of the cover. I got a good look at him as he leaped away. A 311-pound buck was hanging on the meat pole back at camp, but the one that had scented me was larger!

Other mast-bearing species such as hickories can be important. Probably the single greatest environmental catastrophe ever to face eastern wildlife was the loss of the American chestnut. It's been virtually exterminated by an imported fungus. American chestnuts annually produce abundant, highly nutritious mast.

Fruit-bearing hardwoods such as apples, cherries, persimmons and plums can provide an important food source for deer. Whitetails, of course, will feed heavily on the fruit produced by these trees, but the sweet twigs and leaves are also an attraction. In my area, it's safe to say that apples are the undoing of most deer taken by early-season hunters. In years when acorns are scarce, I've also taken a number of late-season deer that couldn't resist walking by an apple tree to see if any fallen fruit remained. Also, young fruit trees — especially those that sprout along orchard boundaries — seem particularly attractive for rubbing.

The last two categories are: general hardwoods like maples, birches, ashes, gums and elms; and evergreen softwoods like pines, spruces, cedars, hemlock, junipers and firs. These can be vitally important at times as food or cover, or ignored at other times.

BEYOND SPECIES

For deer, the size of the tree can have as much or more impact as the species of the tree. Take, for example, the red maple. Young red maples sprouting in cut-over areas are prime deer food. When the trees mature to pole size and the branches have grown out of reach of a browsing deer, they are often rubbed by bucks — the bright white wood under the bark makes a strong visual signpost identifying a buck's presence. A mature red maple has little interest to deer, unless it falls or is cut so that the top buds again are in reach for browsing.

Likewise, some young evergreens are used for food, some are preferred rub species and others are critical winter cover in deer yards. In my hunting area, hemlocks are another species that have large, low-hanging branches, and are a good bet for finding scrapes.

So as you set about dissecting the deer woods in your area, remember that the pieces of information you gather are like the individual pieces of an infinite jigsaw puzzle. Eventually, if you put enough of them together, they will form a picture that is the next buck you'll harvest.

This buck is likely using this maze of dense cover as a sanctuary from hunters and predators. Identify the shrubs as a preferred cover source.

Deer Pelletology

C. J. WINAND

It happens to every hunter at least once in his or her life: that uneasy feeling you get when you realize that the last bean burrito you ate the night before hasn't been sitting too well. It's a pain that hits at 7 a.m. in your treestand.

Since you're already 20 feet in the air, you have two options. You could climb down from your treestand. Or, you could squat down over the edge of your stand (safety harness secured, of course).

A problem develops if you're 20 feet in the air and you realize that there isn't any toilet paper in your pocket; no way to reach all those choice leaves on the ground. Instead of panicking, you draw the trusty Buck knife and cut off the tops of your socks. A T-shirt pocket works, too.

Been there, done that. Most every hunter has gone through something like this. In fact, my good friend, Tony Canami, is one of those guys who has left his mark in every parcel of woods in Harford County, Maryland. You always know Tony has been in the woods by the number of cut-off socks. Since Tony hunts almost every day, hunters in his area can tell where the hotspots are by the number of sock-tops.

But hunters aren't the only ones "going" in the woods. Deer do, too. That's why one day Tony and I were discussing the "science" of deer feces and what it can mean to hunters. Unlike the first few paragraphs, the rest of this story will focus on the art and science of deer "pelletology" from a deer biology and behavior point of view.

Many hunters are probably saying to themselves, "What can I learn from a bunch of deer droppings? Can we actually get closer to deer by learning something about deer pellets? Do all deer defecate in the same area? Are buck droppings larger than does'?" Surprisingly enough, all of these questions have been answered within the scientific community.

WHAT DROPPINGS TELL US

Whenever we come across a pile of droppings, the shape can give hunters many clues as to what the deer have been eating. Generally, round, individual droppings indicate that deer are foraging primarily on leaves, browse and twigs. Pellets clumped together suggest deer have focused their attention on grasses and forbs.

Many hunters have claimed that they can determine the sex of the deer from the size of individual droppings. Research analyzing pellets from penned deer suggests the opposite. In fact, some of the trophy deer droppings I've observed have come from penned does. An exception occurs when you have bucks 4½ years old or older in your area. However, considering that most of the country supports high percentages of younger bucks, betting that the large droppings you've found will lead you to a record-book buck wouldn't be wise.

Way back in 1940, researcher Logan Bennett came up with an idea that is still used in today's deer management. He found that deer defecate 13 times per day. It's no wonder some hunters say they can actually smell deer! And if you're wondering if those large piles are from bucks, biologists have found that some adult bucks do, in fact, produce more pellets per group. Studies also indicate that 75 is the average number of pellets per group. (Can you imagine the poor soul who had to count through all those samples?) So the next time you wander onto a Boone-and-Crockett poop pile, you just might be a short distance "behind" a deer of a lifetime.

■■■

"Studies indicate that 75 is the average number of pellets per group. (Can you imagine the poor soul who had to count through all those samples?)"

■■■

PELLETS AS POPULATION INDICATORS

Another important question that deer hunters always ask biologists is, "How many deer are there in this area?" The answer, or at least a very close approximation, can be found in the number of droppings in the area. In fact, pellet counts are used by many state wildlife departments as a component to estimating deer populations.

Bennett and other biologists determined the defecation rate for deer by walking various transects along a one-square-mile area and counting every pile of "woodland nuggets." Hunters can easily do the same, and those in the North would be advised to conduct this population index every 24 hours after a snowfall. For example: If, after one day, you count 169 drop-

pings along your transects, simply divide by 13. The density of deer within your hunting area is 13 deer per square mile. As with any population index, the more times you sample your area, the more accurate your results.

Other researchers have found that deer might average more piles of dung in the spring and fall. This is probably due to the increasing amounts of fiber added to the bulk feces between spring and fall. Evidently, as the diet changes from succulent leaves and forbs in spring to mature vegetation in summer to more coarse items in fall after leaf-drop, the number of pellet groups increases.

Whenever you find a lot of deer pellets in a relatively small area, you've ventured close to one of two areas . . . the feeding or bedding area. Since bedding areas are always hard to locate and you don't want to push deer from their beds, feces can be a great sign giving away a buck's bedroom.

PELLETS AS COVER SCENT

Another field clue we can identify from pellets is the specific type of forage that deer are keying on right now. With a little practice you'd be surprised at how well you can identify the different plant and mast species. And, since you're already picking through them, I'd suggest rolling and/or rubbing around in deer pellets if it's hunting season. I'd better repeat this . . . rub them all over your hunting clothing. Before you think this is a crazy idea, hear me out.

Did you ever wonder why a dog will roll all over a dead rabbit or opossum? Instinctively, if he knows that he can cover his predator scent with that of another prey species, he will become a more efficient predator. Hunters who step in cow manure (on purpose) or roll or rub deer pellets onto their clothing and

Individual droppings indicate that deer are feeding heavily on leaves and woody browse. Clumped droppings suggest grasses and forbs are the primary forage.

Fresh droppings can help you pinpoint areas with the best deer activity . . . possibly even a buck's bedroom.

■■■

"Hunters who step in cow manure (on purpose) or roll or rub deer pellets onto their clothing and treestand can effectively cover some of their predator odors. Since droppings are located almost everywhere and they're free, hunters can't ask for a better cover scent."

■■■

treestand can effectively cover some of their predator odors. Since droppings are located almost everywhere and they're free, hunters can't ask for a better cover scent.

To prove this point, another biologist and I took droppings from one deer pen and placed them on the ground of a separate pen containing different deer. The results were very interesting. The typical response included a monarch doe and its fawns approaching to investigate the strange droppings, smelling them and simply continuing on with their feeding. They did not become alarmed. Obviously, our next test was on wild, free-ranging deer. Just like the penned deer, the wild deer checked out the unfamiliar odor but did not exhibit any alarm behavior. Before conducting these tests, we hypothesized that, since penned and wild deer were able to identify other individual deer within the herd by smell, the scent of droppings from a foreign deer might cause some degree of fear among the local deer. This definitely was not the case. We also wondered what type of behavioral responses we would observe if we used urine and feces from other species.

Before we could actually test our hypothesis, I discovered an actual "feces thesis" done by researcher Howard Steinberg. Steinberg tested the response from deer encountering feces from other herbivores (vegetarians), omnivores (both vegetation and meat eaters) and carnivores (meat eaters). He found that deer had the greatest aversion toward the feces of carnivores from animals like timber wolves, dogs, bobcats and cougars. Interestingly, no matter how many times the carnivore samples were presented, the deer always exhibited alarm behavior. What about the other samples? Deer showed some aversion to the omnivores, but not as much as the carnivores and hardly any avoidance of feces from herbivores.

The most important finding in these studies has been that deer showed the greatest interest in the pellets from deer of separate herds. Whenever you hunt an area, it's wise to collect those special little woodland nuggets in a plastic bag and use them near your stand in a different hunting area. Since deer are generally curious animals, this technique could be the final trick you need to bag your deer.

THE FINAL WORD

Despite the sometimes humorous tone of this article, deer "pelletology" should be taken seriously by whitetail hunters. We spend a lot of time analyzing the particulars of deer sign like rubs and scrapes. But there are a lot more deer pellets in the woods revealing clues about deer behavior. If you understand how to read all forms of deer sign, you'll be a better hunter. And that's what the science of deer hunting is all about.

Aging Yearlings

C. J. WINAND

One of my first assignments in the wildlife management field occurred at a deer check station. It was a memorable experience.

A hunter explained to us that if you cut off a deer's front leg, you can count the rings in the leg bone and tell how old the deer is. Believe it or not, he was serious; so I tried to explain to him how biologists really age deer . . . their teeth. I always wondered how biologists aged deer so fast at the check station. Well, it's a relatively simple process.

When you harvest a deer, simply look down its mouth and count back to the third tooth on either side of the lower jaw. This tooth, known as the third premolar, is the key to aging yearling deer. If the tooth has three cusps or sections, then you know that the deer is 1½ years old. If the third tooth has two cusps, the deer is one year and seven months old or older. For the rest of the deer's life the third tooth will have two cusps.

After checking the third premolar, biologists study the condition of the other teeth to determine a deer's age. As with anything, experience is the key to precisely aging older deer. Even if you can't peg the exact ages of older deer, why not impress your buddies by picking out those yearlings? Since 70 percent of all bucks harvested in this country are yearlings, odds are good that you'll run across a lot of them.

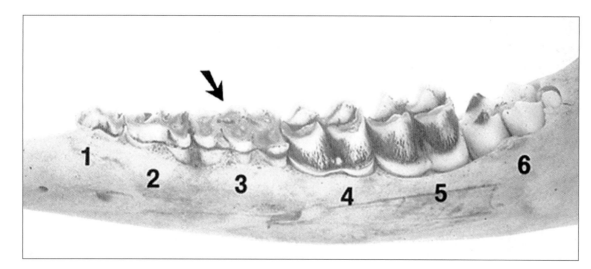

This jawbone comes from a 1½-year-old deer as seen by the three cusps.

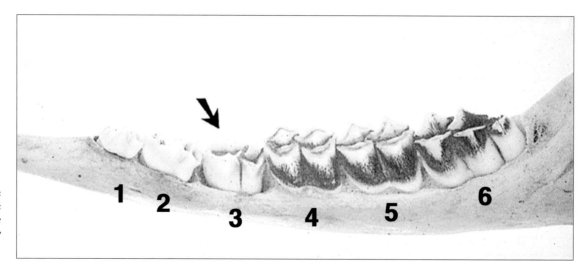

When a deer reaches 1 year and 7 months of age or older, the third tooth has only two cusps.

Under Pressure

JEFF SAMSEL

Raccoon hunters and a pack of hounds singing the songs of sweet-hot scent must be enough to turn the local whitetails inside out, right? Besides the racket, there's the strong stench of human hunters and crazed 'coon hounds that likely lingers well into the morning hours. Surely, the deer will dive into bedding cover. And if you're the deer hunter with access to this same property, you'd probably steer clear that next morning if you knew hunters and hounds had been there the night before.

HERE'S WHAT YOU MISSED:

Nearby, a timer-rigged camera at the edge of a baited field serves as our deer hunter in this test of the effects of raccoon hunting pressure on whitetail movement. Photos are snapped every 15 minutes for the first two and last two hours of daylight on days prior to and after each raccoon hunt. Researchers believe these images will reveal what a deer hunter's odds are of taking a deer the day after the raccoon hunters and hounds have been in the woods.

Twenty-seven deer in the area, a 7,769-acre tract in South Carolina's Low Country, were fitted with radio collars so researchers could track the animals before, during and after each raccoon hunt. Only half the land, designated the "treatment area," was open to the raccoon hunters, so researchers could make comparisons to deer movements on an undisturbed tract. The side used as the treatment area alternated from one week's raccoon hunt to the next.

This study, with weekly hunts from mid-December to February over two seasons, showed that raccoon hunting with trained dogs has no statistically significant effect on deer movements. Thus, according to the study, deer hunters are just as likely to harvest a deer the morning following a raccoon hunt as the morning before.

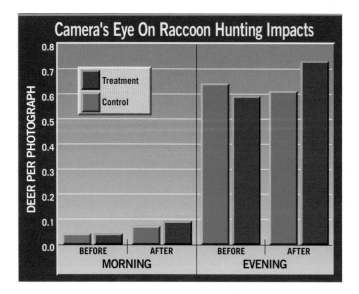

Camera's Eye On Raccoon Hunting Impacts

DEER PER PHOTOGRAPH

Treatment
Control

0.8
0.7
0.6
0.5
0.4
0.3
0.2
0.1
0.0

BEFORE   AFTER   BEFORE   AFTER
    MORNING   EVENING

"Researchers observed no significant changes in the behavior of these deer," according to Buddy Baker, furbearer project supervisor for the South Carolina Department of Natural Resources. "The radio-collared deer continued to move at the same times of the day and in the same general areas despite raccoon hunting the evening before."

The cameras captured roughly the same number of deer in photos taken before and after hunts. In fact, while the differences were insignificant, there were actually more deer per photo in "morning after" shots from the treatment (hunted) area than the control area.

As one might suspect, this study resulted from perceived conflicts between deer hunters and raccoon hunters who often carry out their respective sports on the same land. Due to concerns regarding reduced deer movements caused by raccoon hunters and their dogs, many deer hunting clubs have traditionally not allowed raccoon hunting on their land until after the close of deer season. In fact, on the tract where the study took place, raccoon hunting had previously been allowed but not until after deer season had closed.

A brochure detailing the project's final report explains, "Raccoon hunters, deer hunters and state natural resources departments wanted scientific data to determine the impact, if any, of raccoon hunting upon deer. The study objectives were: to determine the impacts of raccoon hunting activity on deer home ranges and activity patterns; and to determine the impact of raccoon hunting on deer harvest potential."

Even though the research was conducted in South Carolina, it has applications for any states where raccoon hunting is popular and seasons overlap significantly with liberal deer seasons. Raccoon hunters in many states anxiously awaited the results of the study, according to Steve Fielder, field operations manager for the United Kennel Club.

HERE'S WHAT REALLY HAPPENS

"Based on the results of this study, we see no reason deer hunters and raccoon hunters cannot share common hunting grounds,"

Baker concluded. The study was funded by the South Carolina DNR, Westvaco Corporation, South Carolina Coonhunters Association and the State Coonhunters Association Network. Clemson University also participated in the study, which was conducted on Westvaco's North Whitener Tract in Jasper County, South Carolina.

Although this study was carried out to look at specific issues, any research that looks at whitetail movements should be of interest to all deer hunters. One significant finding from this study was that none of the deer, at any time during the tracking periods, ever left its normal home range. Even one deer that was chased by the dogs stayed within its normal range and returned to its bedding area within a few hours.

This is consistent with findings from four unrelated previous research projects that used dogs to run deer directly. In these studies, deer that did leave their home range normally returned within 24 hours of the chase and always within 72 hours.

In the South Carolina study, eight deer were spotted by the raccoon hunters on five separate occasions while the hunters were following baying dogs. In each case, the deer were either bedded down or standing still and either remained where they were or moved off slowly.

"These animals don't move nearly as much as most hunters think they do," said Charles Ruth, deer project supervisor for the South Carolina DNR. "They have established that home

Raccoon hunting and other forms of small-game hunting don't impact deer movement and habits nearly as much as we might expect.

Researchers count on technology to learn more about deer movement tendencies. Remote cameras and radio collars track deer movement.

range for a reason. It has the food they need, and they know where to go to escape danger. They avoid problems by staying close to home."

Still, anyone who does most of his hunting on public land, or even on heavily hunted club land, knows that whitetails become more and more difficult to spot as the season progresses. The weeks surrounding the rut seem to be the only obvious exception. During the rest of the season, deer often show a shift toward nocturnal behavior, limiting most of their travel to nighttime hours. However, the South Carolina study shows that this nocturnal activity often begins just early enough for hunters to take advantage.

THE AFTERNOON AFTER

Afternoon hunts near food sources showed particular promise, according to some of the data gathered in the raccoon hunting study. Of 2,530 deer photographed by 14 self-timed cameras, 2,341 showed up in photos taken during the afternoon, compared to only 189 deer from morning shots. All cameras were located on game patches and in wooded areas baited with corn.

This data was gathered by North American Hunting Club Member Jim Westerhold for his master's thesis. His thesis also noted that photos shot in the afternoon consistently captured more whitetails as it got closer to dark. The last shot taken each day contained an average of more than two deer per frame, while the first of each afternoon, just two hours earlier, averaged one deer per 10 frames — a 20-fold difference.

Based on findings that night raccoon hunting had no affect on the ability of hunters to observe and potentially harvest

deer in the same general area the following day, researchers recommend that raccoon hunters, using trained raccoon hounds, be allowed access to properties being hunted for deer. In fact, other forms of small-game hunting might not have negative impacts on deer hunters either. Westerhold believes that NAHC members shouldn't be discouraged if rabbit, squirrel or bird hunters have been through the area earlier.

"My theory is that it wouldn't change the harvest potential of the deer if the (small game) hunting activity is not happening at the same time (you're out deer hunting)," Westerhold says. "A day in advance or even hours in advance (is enough time for deer to recover). In most cases, we found that deer confronted by dogs don't move until the last instant."

Remote cameras can capture deer activity around the clock.

CHAPTER 3

Hunting Whitetails: Techniques & Tactics

I f you're a whitetail junkie on a quest for a better way to use scents to your advantage, eliminate odor altogether, find bucks when hunting pressure is high, grunt up a buck or learn more about deer vocalizations, you're in the right place.

Now if you read a lot about deer hunting, you've likely received a very healthy dose of this type of advice. As whitetail populations have spread across the country, so has information and misinformation about hunting tactics — so much so that it's easy to get confused about what works and what doesn't.

So if you've found yourself up a tree with four grunt calls slung about your neck, three types of rattling devices hanging within arm's reach, 16 scent bombs dangling within 30 yards, a mock scrape at the head of a mock rub line and a small herd of deer decoys assembled nearby, you're probably relying too much on "hocus-pocus" and not enough on solid, simple hunting techniques and tactics.

Here is selected material from proven writers and hunters — ideas we're confident will truly help you hunt better and smarter. These stories, though, are not the final word on any of these topics. When it comes to deer hunting techniques and tactics, rules are meant to be broken. So beware the buddy who tells you "this is how it is" on whitetail hunting.

And this season, try to travel a little lighter to your deer stand . . .

■ ■ ■

Early Season Feeding Frenzy

JIM CASADA

Mention "mast" to the average deer hunter, and immediately his thoughts turn to acorns. There is no denying the importance of oak mast, but acorns are not necessarily the food item of first choice for deer in the fall. Indeed, where they are available, several of the foodstuffs collectively referred to as "soft mast" take first place on a whitetail's dinner plate.

Perhaps the first point to be made about soft mast is that it will be crucial to your hunting strategy only if available when the hunting season is open. Since the soft mast availablity varies greatly depending on where you live and hunt, as well as with the individual mast item, it is a consideration to keep in mind before you begin tactical planning on stand placement.

DEER CANDY

A good place to start when it comes to soft mast is with the various fruits that hunters sometimes refer to as "deer candy." Anywhere there are deer and bearing autumn fruit trees, the deer will quickly zero in on the ripening and falling apples and pears. Find a consistently productive apple or pear tree on an abandoned farm or in a remote pasture and you'll have a prize hunting spot. Pears are a bit more predictable in bearing fruit thanks to hardiness and less likelihood of a late frost killing the blooms. These fruits virtually guarantee a feeding frenzy at ripening time, and if that comes during a period when you can hunt, you'll be wise to take advantage of the opportunity.

Indeed, some shrewd hunters I know go a step further and actively cultivate the fruit trees when they find them. It's a good idea to keep other vegetation cleared away from apples and pears and perhaps even do a bit of pruning in late winter to enhance fruit production next year. (Be sure to check the regulations on baiting in your state and follow the requirements.) In some cases, state game departments have planted fruit trees on public hunting lands or they maintain existing trees.

As the fruits start dropping, deer will make daily feeding trips to enjoy the juicy offerings. On many occasions, I've seen deer stand on their back legs to reach an apple still dangling on the tree. In some areas, apples and pears have come and gone before the season is open, but in others you can enjoy several weeks of bow or gun hunting near fruit trees. Some varieties of apples cling stubbornly to limbs, not falling until long after all leaves are gone. If you know of such a tree, it can be a great place to hunt on the day following a storm or strong winds. Deer seem to have a knack of knowing that the foul weather will have knocked delicious fruit tidbits to the ground.

Apples are prime soft mast, and whitetails love them. Try "sweetening the pot" by knocking down a few treats for area deer.

Another early-season delight for deer is wild grapes and their close kin, scuppernongs and muscadines. In one form or another these are widespread across much of the country, and a lot of varieties of wild grapes ripen in early fall. When they do, deer are greatly attracted to them, and for bowhunters this can be quite important.

■■■

"Fortunately, ripe persimmons are slow to fall, in some cases clinging to limbs long after they have matured."

■■■

The grape season is a fairly short one, because usually they ripen and are gone in a period of only two or three weeks. For that brief time, however, they constitute an important item in a deer's diet. This is especially true over the Southeast, where wild grapes are found almost anywhere that there are woods, overgrown fields, fencerows or any type of uncultivated land. Deer seem particularly drawn to the big, individual growing grapes known as scuppernongs and muscadines. Scouting expeditions to old, abandoned farms or homesteads may reveal fruit trees

and an arbor or two of thriving vines (a grape vine can live for a century or more). No matter what location you're in, preseason scouting should include keeping an eye open for grape vines. If they drop fruit during the hunting season, be there.

As attractive as apples, pears and wild grapes can be in places where they are available, they take a distinct second place to another fruit of the land. For deer, the most widespread and appealing of all the fruity candies is the persimmon. A hardy resident of fencerows, overgrown fields and abandoned farmsteads, the persimmon produces small orange-colored globes, often in great abundance, that deer dearly love. Better still, persimmons usually are at their sweetest when hunting season deer activity is at the peak.

Contrary to popular folk wisdom, it is not true that persimmons are inedible until after the first frost. It is usually late October or into November, at the peak of the rut in many hunting areas, before persimmons become sweet. Until the point when they ripen, though, many a city lad visiting country cousins has learned that persimmons have a tartness that gives new meaning to "pucker power." Unlike humans, deer somehow know (probably through smell) when persimmons are ready to eat. And once that happens, they gather at bearing trees as if addicted.

Fortunately, ripe persimmons are slow to fall, in some cases clinging to limbs long after they have matured. As a result, you might be able to hunt this soft mast over a period of several

Identifying Those Deer Delicacies

FRENCH MULBERRIES

Small branched trees of irregular form with rough pinkish brown bark. Leaves are heart-shaped with toothed edges, pointed tips and rough surfaces. Fruit is like a blackberry and colored pinkish to crimson. French Mulberries are good to eat but have a sharp, acidic taste.

PERSIMMON

Tall trees with black or gray bark that's cracked vertically and horizontally to form irregular squares. The pointed leaves are oval, glossy and leathery. Persimmon fruit is about quarter-sized and round. Becomes orange when ripened and sweet to taste.

HONEY LOCUST

Grows as three-spined buds. Leaves are gold in autumn and paired on sides as leaflets. The distinctive seed pod becomes red-brown. It is frequently flat, jointed, thick-edged, curved and twisted and resembles an overgrown green bean. The pod is approximately 16 inches long and one inch wide. The soft, succulent pulp inside is sweet and a major attractor of deer.

SUMAC

This small tree has crimson, plum-shaped fruit clusters that are bright red in the fall. Leaves grow in long clusters with parallel leaflets. Limbs resemble horns of a stag in velvet when growing during early summer. These bushes grow about head-high and deer will break the tops down when feeding on them.

APPLES

Fruit can be baseball size or larger and colored red, yellow or green. Apple orchards have problems with deer in many regions of the country. Old homesteads are good places to look for these trees, which generally fork about head height and have a smooth gray-brown-colored bark.

GRAPES

Both cultivated and wild grapes are deer favorites. The wild version can be found on old farms, forest openings and clearcuts. The vines often climb trees. The fruit is generally dark purple or blue in color and grows in clusters. The feeding season is short, the fruit ripens fast and falls easily.

weeks. However, this is not likely to be the case if the fruits are discovered by opossums, skunks or raccoons. These critters and many others love the tasty treats. For that matter, so do humans. If you've ever been privileged to feast on a properly prepared persimmon pudding, you'll understand why. It is a country-boy gourmet's delight.

Deer hunters owe it to themselves to locate every persimmon tree in the areas they regularly hunt and check them before the season to see if they are bearing mast. If so, make plans to hunt them at the appropriate time. Thanks to the fact that their ripening coincides so closely with the open deer hunting season across wide areas of the country, not to mention just how much deer love the fruit, persimmons deserve more attention than they are sometimes given. They are deer candy at its sweetest, and even the wisest of old bucks is likely to have a sweet tooth.

Take note that many scent manufacturers have recognized the importance of soft mast as an attractant for hungry deer. Examples of the aforementioned soft mast fruits can be purchased as an attractant scent. If you buy and try one, follow the directions and let the deer be the final judge.

MORE MAST

In addition, there are a number of other soft mast items that deserve attention. Among the foods that are noteworthy include: sumac berries, French mulberries (also known as American beauty berry), Osage orange fruits (the tree is known in some areas as bodock), maypops (wild passion fruit), paw-paws and the fruit of the honey locust.

Sumac is easily identified in early fall because of the vivid scarlet of its leaves; the red clusters of berries are also readily visible. It is my personal opinion that deer find several other types of soft mast preferable to sumac, but they eat it regularly. Also, sumac seems to bear every year, a quality that is not true of many other varieties of soft mast. So do French mulberries, which are easily spotted thanks to their vivid pinkish purple color. Whitetails eat the berries of this low-growing plant and also find the tips of its limbs quite desirable.

The Osage orange bears huge, rough-skinned, baseball-sized fruits, and deer often will nibble on them when they are available. As with sumac, though, it does not seem to be a preferred food item. Much the same is true of passion fruit, although deer will break open the yellow balls of this ground vine to get at the pulp inside.

On the other hand, when it comes to paw-paws, a musky-tasting fruit with something of a resemblance to the smell and taste of a banana, deer love them. Unfortunately, paw-paws are rather rare, being found mostly in rich ground where there is plenty of moisture. However, if you can identify the fruit and know where several plants are located, rest assured that the deer know that location also.

HONEY LOCUST HONEYHOLE

To me, the pods of the honey locust might be the most overlooked of all the types of soft mast. They grow on the variety of locust that is adorned with the long, sharp thorns dreaded by hunters. Once leaves have fallen, the brown leathery pods are easily spotted. They normally do not begin dropping until well into November. It seems that they offer deer a sweet treat when most similar items are no longer available. Just pick up a recently fallen locust pod and peel away the covering to get at the fleshy area around the seeds. One taste will tell you why the word "honey" goes with this species of locust. It will also explain why old-timers sometimes brewed a sweet-tasting beer from the pods.

Deer dine on the seed pods daintily, munching only the portion that's meaty, and when they are through the leftovers are somewhat reminiscent of the rinds remaining after a summertime watermelon feast. Honey locust trees are often found standing alone, and if you have one covered with pods, it's a fine place to be hunting when they begin to fall.

CONCLUSION

Soft mast is almost never as abundant as hard mast, but the fact that many types are particularly appealing to deer makes it important, especially early in the season. The sweetness of the fruits makes them a definite favorite of deer that are loading up for the long winter ahead. Plan your early-season hunts with these considerations in mind and your deer hunting season might end quickly. Then you might have the rest of the fall to hunt all those other game species you've been dreaming about.

This deer candy store of ripened apples is open for business, and the customers have arrived for the feeding frenzy.

Making Sense of Deer Scents

GARY CLANCY

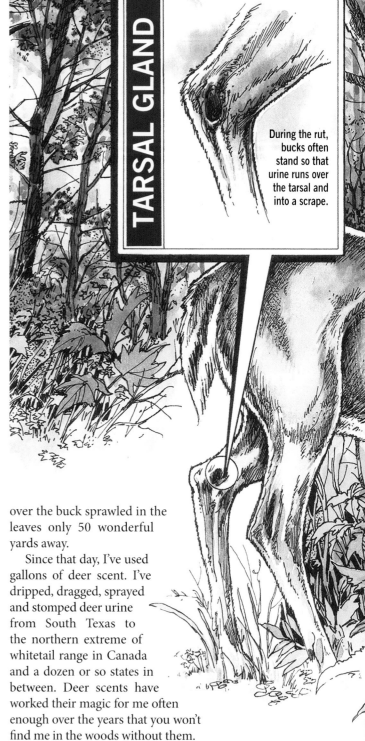

TARSAL GLAND

During the rut, bucks often stand so that urine runs over the tarsal and into a scrape.

Nobody I knew that many years ago used deer scent to improve his odds of bagging a whitetail, but when I plunked down a buck-fifty for the first bottle of deer urine I'd ever seen, I had high hopes.

I spotted it on the counter while selling muskrat hides to the local fur buyer. Three days into the season, I still hadn't the courage to use it. Hey, if it didn't work, I didn't want the guys laughing at the kid in camp for falling for some gimmick. But I was getting desperate. Four bucks hung on the meatpole behind the old cabin; none of them were mine.

So, on that cold November morning, I cracked the cap and poured some of the juice onto the toes of my pac boots. About every 100 steps, I dumped a few more drops. It wasn't pretty. But it's probably the way most deer hunters begin experimenting with deer scents. By the time I got to my stand and went to wipe my nose with the back of my glove, I wondered if more stink was on my hand than my boots.

The first hour that morning was uneventful, just a couple of shots off in the distance. I was about ready to search out a better spot when I heard a buck grunting. The buck's rapid approach grew louder and he was grunting with every breath. I pulled the old pump 12 gauge into position just as the buck — a seven-pointer with a couple of busted tines — hurried over the ridge. With his nose glued to the ground and a good head of steam, I wondered if he'd run right into my tree. I know now that I should have waited, but patience was not one of my strong points.

When my first shot whistled by him, that buck skidded to a halt, lifted his head and looked around wondering what happened. The second ounce of lead slamming into a tree behind him spurred the buck on a mad dash right past my twisted old oak. Four more times I shucked the old pump as the buck blew by. He was gone, and I sat in the tree shaking like a whipped pup.

Ten minutes later, I climbed down from the tree for a look around. I would have bet my shotgun that I'd missed, but Pa was a stickler about not wasting game, and he had taught me to always look for sign of a hit. The half-dozen, scattered, green hulls on the ground, smoking reminders of the debacle, made me sink even lower as I took up the track of the buck. Following the path of his hasty flight was easy across the frosty leaves. When I came upon the crimson splash on both sides of his track, though, I let out a whoop and tracked like a Bluetick pup on a hot coon scent. In my excitement, I nearly tripped

over the buck sprawled in the leaves only 50 wonderful yards away.

Since that day, I've used gallons of deer scent. I've dripped, dragged, sprayed and stomped deer urine from South Texas to the northern extreme of whitetail range in Canada and a dozen or so states in between. Deer scents have worked their magic for me often enough over the years that you won't find me in the woods without them.

Yet, I'll be the first to preach that deer scents won't hide sloppy hunting tactics. What scents can do for you is help you bring in that buck that you otherwise would never see. Used correctly, scents can help mask your own odor and give you those precious extra seconds we so desperately need to get off a good shot. When I'm bowhunting, I use scents to help position the deer right where I want it for the shot. Scents can make a deer decoy smell like the real thing and sometimes work wonders in combination with rattling and calling. But like rattling, calling, decoys and other hunting aids, scents don't work all the time. Expect miracles and you'll quickly become disappointed. Accept scents as another method that can improve your odds

PREORBITAL

This gland and the forehead gland play a role in scent communication at rubs and overhanging branches.

METATARSAL

Produces a scent alerting deer to danger. Hind leg.

INTERDIGITAL

Allows deer to follow one another by scent.

and you'll probably end up like me — checking your pockets to make sure that you have a bottle of scent before heading into the woods.

What should that bottle have in it? Depends on how you're trying to fool the deer's nose.

Back when I began using scents, there were two choices — deer urine and fox urine. I bought fox urine in pint bottles from the fur buyer for years before I ever saw small bottles of fox urine intended for deer hunters. Fox urine was my cover scent and deer urine was the lure. Today's choices are more complex. We writers have contributed to that confusion by grouping scents into only two categories: cover scents and at-

tractants. Scent science becomes clearer if we recognize four categories: cover scents, food attractants, gland-based lures and deer urine.

UNDER COVER

A cover scent is anything that you put on your clothing or near your stand to mask your human odor. Fox urine, coon urine and some tree or earth scents are the most common.

Most of us overdo it with cover scents. A cover scent cannot eliminate your human odor. Instead, it is intended to hide that odor well enough to confuse the olfactory signals that a downwind deer receives. Sometimes it works well enough to allow time for a clean, killing shot. If you take the "more is better"

Proper scent use won't always save you from a downwind deer. It makes sense to position yourself where a buck won't inhale a snout-full of your human odor. The idea behind cover scent is to mask your odor and buy a few extra, precious seconds.

approach and lather on the cover scent, you defeat the purpose. Deer are accustomed to smelling fox urine, for example, in small doses. A couple of drops is all you want.

Though much research has been conducted on the whitetail's senses of sight, smell and hearing, we do not know what deer actually smell when they detect human odor. However, we do know that a deer's sense of smell is at least 10 times better than ours. Researchers also believe that a large portion of a deer's brain is devoted to olfaction. What's more, the whitetail's large nasal lining (epithelium) allows the animal to recognize up to six different odors simultaneously.

APPLE PIE, NOT COW PIE

It's a mistake to lump a bunch of other scents under the category of cover scents when they're really food attractant scents. A partial list would include apple, acorn, sweet corn, honeysuckle and persimmon. The whole idea behind a cover scent is that it be something that the deer is used to smelling and is not attracted to. Smells that deer associate with food defeat the purpose.

Scents like apple and persimmon are intended to attract deer. Don't put them on yourself nor very close to your stand. In-

stead, use food attractant scents in locations around your stand that will help position a deer for a good shot opportunity.

Before using food attractant scents, be sure to check out the laws on baiting in the state you are hunting. In some locations, putting out *anything* that the deer might be inclined to eat qualifies as bait.

GLANDS HOLD SCENT SECRETS

Gland-based lures are the latest craze among deer scent companies. Produced from the tarsal, interdigital, forehead, preorbital or metatarsal gland, each is designed with a specific purpose in mind. Scents that incorporate tarsal gland, for instance, are an excellent choice for doctoring scrapes. The combination of buck urine and tarsal gland mimics the communication behavior of a buck when he squats and urinates over a scrape. Early in the pre-rut, bucks often urinate in scrapes with their legs splayed. However, as the rut gets closer they almost always stand in the scrape with tarsal glands together and urinate through them into the scrape.

My favorite scent system starts with peeling the tarsal glands from a freshly killed rutting buck. If any of my buddies takes a mature, rutting buck before I do, I always go over and have a look, tell him what a dandy the deer is, and make off with the tarsal glands.

I leave one tarsal as is and put the other in a Zip-Loc bag with half an ounce of doe-in-estrus urine. After slicing a hole in each tarsal, I tie them with a string and drag them or sometimes tie one to each boot. I lay down a scent trail while hiking into my stand and will sometimes loop past the stand and back again. This improves the odds of a buck crossing the trail and turning in my direction. Assuming that my stand is facing directly upwind, I hang one tarsal from a bush or limb 20 yards to my right and the other the same distance to my left. Any buck catching a whiff is likely to investigate — especially if I've done an adequate job of eliminating my own human scent. Many times I've witnessed bucks sniff and lick the tarsal glands. One buck even tore a tarsal from the bush where I had hung it. He proceeded to rake the tarsal on the ground with his antlers.

■ ■ ■

Cover scents are not foolproof because a deer's nasal passages are designed in a way that allows them to detect up to six different odors simultaneously.

■ ■ ■

The interdigital gland is small and located between the split hooves of a deer. The gland secretes a waxy substance, and it is believed that scent left from the interdigital gland helps deer follow each other. Thus, scents using the interdigital gland are also great for leaving scent trails you want the deer to follow.

Rubs and the overhanging branch at a scrape are critical visual signposts for deer. But scent at these important locations appears to be at least equally important in whitetail communication. The forehead gland and preorbital gland come into play on rubs and on overhanging branches at scrapes. When a buck rubs a tree with his antlers, the exposed cambium layer of the tree is obvious to the eye. But the scent left by the buck's forehead gland, preorbital gland and even his saliva are the animal's signature — the way he identifies himself to other deer. It's been my experience that bucks are attracted to mock rubs whether or not the rub has been doctored with scent. However, a buck could be enticed to stay in the vicinity longer if a scent is used on the rub.

Basically, the same holds true when using forehead gland and preorbital gland scent on the overhanging branch of mock scrapes or existing scrapes. Many times when a buck comes to a scrape, he focuses most of his attention on the branch rather than the scrape itself.

Early in November one year, I was hunting in western Illinois and made a mock scrape 12 steps in front of my treestand.

I doctored the scrape and overhanging branch with scent. The first day I sat in the stand, six different bucks checked it. All were immature bucks — yearlings and 2½-year-olds. Interestingly, however, none of the six urinated in the scrape or pawed at it. All six, though, smelled and licked the overhanging branch. Four rubbed their faces and antlers on it.

The small metatarsal gland is covered by white hairs and located low on each hind leg. Scent from the metatarsal gland is released only when a deer becomes alarmed. At least one scent manufacturer has taken the metatarsal gland, combined it with human fatty acids and created a scent intended to repel deer. By placing the scent along peripheral trails it is thought that hunters can funnel deer closer to stand locations. Still, some research indicates that the metatarsal gland neither repels nor attracts other whitetails.

DEER URINE SCENTS

This is the largest category of deer scents and the one with which most hunters have had some experience. Buck urine, doe urine, doe-in-estrus urine (often called doe-in-heat scent) and fawn urine are usually sold in liquid form, but you can also find it as a gel, powder, patch, solid wafer or even send it up as smoke or vapor.

There is a common assumption that doe-in-estrus urine should be used only during the rut, while the other urine scents are better suited for use during pre-rut and post-rut. The contention is that using the doe-in-estrus urine at any time other than during the rut will alert rather than attract deer. This assumes that deer know that the time is not right for them to be smelling the scent of an estrous doe and so they become suspicious. I don't buy it.

I've been using doe-in-estrus lures since the 1970s. During that time, I've used them from September to January while hunting whitetails across North America. Never have I seen any evidence of doe-in-estrus lure spooking a buck, regardless of the season. True, I have found these lures to be most effective during the scraping period and actual breeding season, but I've also enjoyed good results long before and long after the rut.

Remember, a white-tailed buck is capable of breeding from the time he sheds the velvet from his antlers right up until he drops his headgear. During that period any buck catching a whiff of doe-in-estrus scent is a candidate for your freezer. I've watched them sniff the scent and ignore it. I've observed as bucks have inhaled the scent, showed mild interest and then went on about their business. And, on many occasions, I've seen them become slaves to the tantalizing aroma. I've never seen it spook them.

The only problem I've ever had while using doe-in-estrus lure has been from does. Often I've had does smell my trail of doe-in-estrus scent and instantly go on full alert. Stomping their front hooves and snorting are other doe behaviors I've witnessed while using doe-in-estrus scent. If a buck is nearby, this can spell disaster. Still, in my experience, the positives have outweighed the negatives.

I don't really see the need for buck urine. You might be able to pique a buck's territorial instincts by laying down a trail of buck urine, but a buck is more inclined to follow a trail of doe-in-estrus than buck urine. Ditto for using buck urine in scrapes. My results with this technique have been disappointing. You can't blame a buck for looking for a receptive doe instead of a fight with another buck.

Scents can help you to see more deer, attract larger bucks, avoid detection by downwind deer, more accurately predict the direction of a deer's approach and position a buck for the shot. Makes sense to experiment with them and learn how to beat a buck's nose.

You don't have to reserve urine attractant scents for the rut. A buck is likely to investigate the scent of another deer at any time during the season.

Decoying Bucks

LARRY WEISHUHN

The use of decoys to dupe white-tailed bucks might seem like a modern deer hunting tactic, but its roots actually date back to the American Indians. Centuries ago, tribesmen used real deer hides, antlers, and even frozen deer heads, to lure rut-crazed bucks into bow range. Modern hunters, however, didn't revive the tactic until the late 1960s.

I happened to be one of those "modern" hunters who inadvertently helped bring decoying back to the forefront of effective tactics for hunting unpressured bucks. It was the autumn of 1969, and I vividly recall that first attempt at constructing (yes, that is correct!) and using a deer decoy.

I spent considerable time building a papier-mâché and styrofoam white-tailed buck, making it as anatomically correct as possible and then painting it to match the colors of the local deer. To top it off, I put an impressive rack on the deer's head and set the "decoy" in an area where I could watch it. My initial purpose was not to attract deer but to catch a poacher who had been trespassing onto private property and killing deer.

Rather than take the decoy home that first night I left it in the field. Before daylight the next morning, I returned to the scene to check the decoy. When I walked to where it had been standing, I found the decoy on the ground looking like it had been shot with buckshot. In the poor, pre-dawn light, I hurriedly set the buck back on its feet.

I stayed in the area all day, but the poacher did not show. Again I left my homemade decoy in the field that night. Next morning, I was again back before daylight, only to find my artistic creation in numerous pieces. At first, I was convinced my decoy had been destroyed by the suspected poacher. But upon inspecting the area more closely, I could see deer tracks all around and large puncture marks all over the decoy's decimated body. It wasn't buckshot that did the damage. It was antlers. The only possible explanation was that a buck had taken great exception to having another buck on his home turf!

Later that same year, I put my decoy back together, set it on the edge of a food plot and shot a buck as it approached the decoy. The buck sidled toward the decoy with all his hair standing on end while he postured aggressively.

At the time, I really didn't think much about using decoys. They were merely something to play with in the fall. Nonetheless, I continued using them for a few years — more as a novelty than anything. Quite frankly, I didn't see much future in using deer decoys for hunting because of the safety factor. But a lot of things have changed.

Today's deer decoys are made of a variety of foams and plastics. Some are made to be easy to carry and simply fold nicely

If a real buck approaches your buck decoy, it's probably the result of aggression. If you don't kill the buck, he might just kill your decoy.

A doe decoy doctored with doe-in-heat scent can be a deadly combination that some bucks can't resist.

nore buck decoys and are not really attracted to nor frightened by them. Reactions to doe decoys have also been interesting.

I often doctor doe decoys by applying a doe-in-heat scent. Frequently, this has helped lure curious bucks even closer to my position. Reports from many other avid whitetail hunters I know confirm the effectiveness of this tactic. If you're hunting solely for a buck, I'd recommend using this approach. If, however, you want a doe decoy to lure antlerless deer when you have an antlerless-only or either-sex tag, I'd avoid it. It seems that once a white-tailed doe encounters a doe decoy doctored with doe-in-heat scent, she'll avoid the area. This is the case primarily because other does do not particularly want to be around a doe that is in estrus.

Remember, white-tailed deer are individuals. Some are attracted to certain stimuli while others aren't. During the fall, bucks are also extremely moody with these swings brought on by hormonal changes. One moment a mature buck might be extremely aggressive toward another buck, the next moment he might approach and check out a new buck in the area while exhibiting no aggressive behavior whatsoever. If a third buck wanders by, the original buck, which has exhibited both aggressive and curious behavior, might become entirely disinterested and not give the other a second look. This is why, even in regions where there is a narrow buck-to-doe ratio and the rut is at the right stage, some days you can rattle in bucks and other days you cannot. But deer are also, by nature, fairly curious. Decoys capitalize on this.

■ ■ ■

"Like most deer hunting techniques, decoys are dynamite some days and disaster on others. I'm still trying to figure out if there are any environmental factors that affect how whitetails will respond to decoys."

■ ■ ■

I frequently use a foam doe decoy when hunting on private property. I like the convenience of being able to roll it up and stick it in a daypack when moving from rattling site to rattling site. Frankly, I use the decoy as a confidence decoy more than an attractant, even though I douse it with doe-in-heat scent. When a buck responds to rattling, he sees another "deer" and concentrates on it more than looking for movement, or looking for an excuse to quickly leave the area. The decoy generally affords me a little more time to evaluate the buck's rack and determine his age.

In setting up a decoy, be it laying down or standing up, always take into consideration wind direction and sun position. I generally set it upwind of my position if I'm hunting from a

into a backpack, other manufacturers produce rigid 3-D or 2-D decoys.

SAFETY FIRST

In using any kind of deer decoy the key word is caution. Our current "crop" is so lifelike, they will not only occasionally fool a deer, but a hunter as well. I strongly recommend never using a deer decoy when hunting in a public hunting area or where you are not certain as to the location of every hunter on the property. Even if you know the other hunters and where they'll be hunting, you should make a point of alerting them that you'll be using a decoy near your stand. Never carry a decoy out of the woods unless it has been dismantled and/or it is completely covered with blaze-orange material.

Keeping safety issues in mind, I've used deer decoys for a long time. And during those many years, I've been fortunate to witness some unique deer behaviors because of it. But like most deer hunting techniques, decoys are dynamite some days and disaster on others. I'm still trying to figure out if there are any environmental factors that affect how whitetails will respond to decoys. So far, no real pattern has emerged.

USING DECOYS

Still, there are some general consistencies that exist. In my experience, white-tailed bucks exhibit aggressive behaviors when they encounter a buck decoy. Does, on the other hand, often ig-

Though the doe seems unimpressed by the buck decoy, this big buck figures he's worth checking out. The decoy has done its job by capturing the buck's attention and allowing the hunter time for a shot.

blind or slightly quartering downwind if rattling. Bucks generally respond to rattling by circling the sound and coming in downwind. You should set a buck decoy so that it is quartering toward your stand position because a buck will likely confront the decoy face to face. Do the reverse with a doe decoy so that you'll get a quartering away shot in either case.

Another decoy positioning tactic is especially effective for deer hunters trying to take whitetails from areas that feature

Bucks will usually approach a doe decoy from the rear and a buck decoy head-on.

expansive stretches of heavy brush. Imagine this type of setting with small open areas. Most of the deer trails are found inside the brushy areas, where it's too thick for a bullet or arrow to penetrate. Cribbing can pull deer out of the thick stuff just long enough for you to make a clean kill.

Cribbing is simply placing the decoy broadside right against the edge of the dense brush. Look for the place where the brush is heaviest so a whitetail can't investigate the decoy from within the cover. This forces the deer to expose itself in order to confront the decoy. Obviously, it's better in this type of situation, where the deer's vision is limited, to choose a full-body or 2-D standing decoy rather than a foam, bedded deer decoy.

Where it is legal and safe to do so, using a deer decoy, buck or doe, becomes another tool to help you harvest a white-tailed deer. But decoying deer is not an end-all secret to taking monster bucks. As I mentioned, some days bucks will respond and investigate decoys; other days they will not. The biggest secrets to taking deer are to go hunting, hunt hard all day long and to be prepared when the moment of truth arrives. Your bag of tricks, however, is certainly more complete if it includes a deer decoy.

Talking Deer

LARRY WEISHUHN

Think back to last deer season and answer honestly. Did you actually hear a deer make a vocalization other than a "snort" as it spooked?

I'm not surprised. We hunters are becoming much more conscious of what happens in the deer woods. We also understand whitetails better than we ever have.

This rare photo captures a buck making the aggressive snort-wheeze vocalization.

There was a time not long ago when most hunters and even biologists did not believe that deer made any vocalizations beyond the snort, most frequently heard as an alarm call. Times certainly have changed.

LISTENING TO DEER

Back in the late 1960s, I worked with penned whitetails as part of my duties as the assistant project leader of Texas' wildlife disease project. In our pens at Texas A&M University we maintained about 100 deer throughout the year. While conducting research and caring for the deer, I listened to does vocalize to their fawns in the spring and summer. I heard bucks grunt as the breeding season approached. When I mentioned these vocalizations to some of the more learned researchers of the time, they simply laughed at me.

Undaunted, whenever I went deer hunting I did my best to imitate those short, guttural grunting sounds made by bucks. Sometimes a combination of rattling and grunting did the trick. Other times, grunting worked on its own. Had I been more enterprising, I might have tried to design a call that replicated sounds similar to those that the deer in our pens made. Frankly, I was satisfied to imitate those sounds and call deer with my mouth. After all, everyone back then knew deer didn't make any sounds! Since then we've learned that whitetails are quite vocal, especially during the fall as the rut approaches.

HOW TO TALK TO DEER

These days it seems you're not a whitetail hunter unless you have a grunt tube or two hanging around your neck. Deer respond to calls made by hunters that duplicate those sounds real deer make and other calls that spark the animal's curiosity.

To illustrate the latter, on several occasions I have taken youngsters deer hunting with me. Kids are easily bored when nothing shows. To make the hunting experience more fun, I allow them to blow on a grunt call. Sometimes the sounds that come out don't in any way resemble those made by a deer. Yet, quite often such "interesting" calls attract bucks and does. There is no way to explain why deer respond to such sounds other than purely out of curiosity. But you better not depend upon a deer to respond to your calls because it's curious! It's far better to learn some of the basics of calling deer and do your best to duplicate those sounds.

During the fall, bucks are very vocal. Often, as a buck travels through the woods, it will grunt softly and look around to see if another deer is watching or will respond. Then the buck will take a few steps, grunt again, watch and listen. A buck will sometimes continue this calling until it reaches its destination whether it's a feeding or bedding area. Essentially, that deer is telling all the bucks within earshot that he is tough and mean, ready to take on all comers. At the same time the buck is communicating its dominance to the does in the area.

I've often heard bucks grunting as they walk toward a choice feeding area, or while heading toward a scrape. By duplicating this short, soft "eck" sound while heading to an area I planned to rattle, I've had bucks follow me. I suspect that they were coming to see what kind of buck walked through the area.

When bucks (especially yearlings) chase does, quite often they grunt a series of "ecks," one with each step they take. While hunting whitetails in the South, I've heard bucks coming my way long before I could see them. I frequently use these short but repetitive grunts when sitting in a stand and shortly after a doe has just walked past.

Both of these calls can easily be duplicated by using various commercial grunt calls, as can the snort calls. I use the latter frequently when I'm "blown" at by a doe or unseen deer that has caught my scent or suspects something is not quite right. I respond in kind with a snort, hopefully to dupe the attentive deer into thinking that I'm another deer. Sometimes it works, sometimes it doesn't. But it's worth a try.

The most aggressive vocalization made by a buck is the snort-wheeze. This call is most often made just before two bucks fight or immediately after by the winner of a fight. The snort-wheeze can only be made with your mouth.

It partially sounds something like the spitting sound made by a cat, followed by a long drawn out hiss — a rapid "fit, fit, fit" followed by a drawn out "ffffeeeeeeeeeeeeeeeeeeee." To make the sound, put your lower lip against the upper front teeth and blow three rapid "fit" sounds, with your tongue against the roof of your mouth. Immediately after making these sounds, draw air through a small space between your tongue and palate, making a hissing and slightly gurgling sound. Use this aggressive vocalization just before rattling during the tail end of the pre-rut and during the heat of the rut.

GETTING AGGRESSIVE

Although deer vocalizations have not changed in thousands of years, modern hunters have just recently learned how to capitalize on the whitetail's complex communication system. Basic grunt calls were popularized in the 1970s and '80s. In the 1990s, call makers perfected such products as the estrous bleat call and the grunt-snort-wheeze. Within the past few years, hunters have enjoyed increased success with new calls designed to mimic emotionally charged rutting bucks.

These new calls imitate the growl, roar or "beller" of a mature buck that is in hot pursuit of an estrous doe. The vocalization includes a deep, resonating string of intense clicking grunts that rise in cadence and end in a sound similar to an exasperated bawl. Bucks will also make this sound when trying to fend off other bucks that are vying for the same doe.

Hunters who don't carry a grunt call afield handicap themselves.

Again, the vocalization itself is not new. In fact, the "buck beller" was documented in wildlife behaviorists' journals as far back as the late 1950s.

Whitetails in many ways are like people. Some seem to never shut up. Others seldom say anything, but when they do it's best to listen. I mentioned earlier that we had a lot of deer in our research pens. Not only did I have the chance to listen to bucks vocalize during the rut, I also paid attention to does throughout the year.

A couple of the does in our facility seemed to almost constantly make some sort of vocalization throughout most of the year, except as the rut approached. At that point, body language was their primary form of communication.

When you are in the field take the time to listen carefully to the sounds whitetails make. Usually, the vocalizations are very soft and quiet. But if you're a good listener, you'll learn how to speak the whitetail's language.

A Level Playing Field

LAURIE LEE DOVEY

Walking the edge of a thick, Southern palmetto swamp, I had to laugh to myself. These woods looked like they'd already been decorated for Christmas; hundreds of strands of flagging tape hanging tinsel-like from eye-level limbs. A lot of hunters still don't use or trust a compass, and many haven't yet bought a global positioning system (GPS). But if you're going to mine southern flatlands and swamps—any flatlands and swamps for that matter—for old, mossy-antlered bucks, you better know how to find your way. And you'll have to learn how the deer find their way from food to bed. If you don't get lost, you're well on your way to what can be excellent deer hunting. But you'll have to break through the boredom of hunting country that, from the outside, "all looks the same."

Few know how to attack and conquer the flats more successfully than master woodsman and deer hunter Terry Rohm. When Rohm moved to Georgia from Pennsylvania, he had to learn, through the School of Hard Knocks, how to effectively dissect the foreign southern terrain—mostly vast expanses of flat land. Vast, flat expanses like this are common in many other whitetail regions as well— notably in Texas and the northwoods of Minnesota and Wisconsin, to name a couple. Today, Rohm, a resident of Madison, Georgia, knows the ways of whitetails on the flats. His experience pays big-buck dividends each year at home and in the other regions mentioned, as well as Mississippi and Kansas, where the words "ridge" and "draw" are rarely part of the local vocabulary.

"Flatland hunters lose two advantages that high-country sportsmen count on—landmark references and long-range visibility," Rohm says. "Mountain ridges that help hunters easily find their way through the wilderness and often dictate wildlife travel routes are gone. In addition, vantage points along ridges that allow hunters to observe vast expanses of land are unavailable. This requires a more intense scouting program that helps hunters become intimately familiar with the land they're hunting. They must learn to identify areas frequented by deer and pinpoint high-percentage hunting areas within the flat woods, fields and wetlands."

THE FLATLANDS HUNTER'S TOOLS

Rohm believes that a number of tools should be standard equipment in any flatland hunter's daypack: aerial photographs, a topographical map, a compass and a hand-held GPS unit. Even though you might have read about and considered all these items before, a short walk into the flats is all it takes to prove how valuable this gear becomes in the South.

Topographical maps take you one step further and serve as an on-the-ground guide and journal of information gathered while scouting. Deer travel routes, main creek crossings, various food sources and preferred bedding areas all can be marked on the map. Combine the topo map with a compass. The compass serves as a travel guide and provides critical information for expeditious and safe travel in and out of the wilderness. A compass is also critical in choosing a direction of travel that works prevailing winds so that potential hunting areas aren't contaminated with human scent. You might not need a compass to hunt deer in small fields and woodlots, but you'll rely on it in monotonous wooded flats and wet swamps that can sprawl for thousands of acres.

■■■

"Standard equipment in any flatland hunter's daypack: aerial photographs, a topographical map, a compass and a hand-held GPS unit."

■■■

A quality hand-held GPS unit can be the flatland hunter's most crucial piece of equipment. GPS technology has improved greatly over the past few years, and units have become extremely user-friendly. The best GPS units for deer hunting are models that feature MicroSD card slots, because this allows the hunter to plug in different maps for their hunting areas. Also look for a unit with an electronic compass. This allows you to take a directional bearing while you are sitting in your treestand or blind. Older units required you to be moving to obtain an accurate compass reading.

Other useful features for today's GPS units include enhanced satellite acquisition and FRS/GMRS radio capabilities, which allows two-way radio communication.

THE NATURE OF FLATLAND DEER

"Deer living in flatland regions are wanderers," Rohm explains. "Although their travels are somewhat affected by habitat and water, their travel paths usually are less predictable than those of mountain region deer. In mountainous terrain, patterning deer movement is often aided by the rugged terrain. Deer might traverse a high ridge to get from a bedding area to a food source. Often those travel trails are used by large numbers of animals and are well defined. On flatlands, deer might travel any one of various routes from the bedding site to a food source. As a result, flatland hunters must be prepared to wander as well and must use other keys and known elements when attempting to pattern the deer."

Rohm's reference to "mountain region deer" simply illustrates how dramatically hilly terrain differs from the flats. But like a lot of deer hunters living across the whitetail's range,

Always carry a GPS unit when hunting any flat country, anywhere. It's easy to get "mixed up" when there aren't elevations or landforms to guide your travels.

Aerial photographs provide a wide-angle, bird's-eye view of the hunting lands. This means quick identification of habitat types, potential feeding, bedding and watering spots and probable travel corridors. Just as important, hunters can pinpoint large blocks of habitat that will likely be unproductive. Think of a flats area as a huge lake. A glance at the lake's surface reveals little if anything about where the fish congregate. Aerial photos are a deer hunter's sonar, detailing important structure and habitat that lies below.

Rohm believes that food sources are the primary key to patterning flatland deer. It just requires a different twist. By starting at a food source and tracking sign away from the food source, Rohm can begin to identify patterns.

"Finding food sources isn't as easy as we might think because preferred food sources change during the hunting season," Rohm explains. "Defining the food sources available and knowing which are preferred by deer at various times during the season is critical to scouting and hunting success." Rohm recommends talking to biologists and learning as much as possible about what the habitat offers in the way of food types. Rohm also walks creeks to locate favored crossing points where deer traffic is funneled. From a heavily used crossing area, Rohm branches out following tracks and other sign that can lead him to bedding areas or food sources.

"In most cases, sign around a prime food source or key creek crossing is heavy," Rohm admits. "As you travel away from the sites, sign begins to diminish at the points where the deer disperse. When sign becomes more difficult to follow, I implement one of two scouting plans."

"When traveling toward a known bedding area or food source, I follow sign as far as I can," he continues. "When the sign dwindles, I travel in the direction that I believe the deer would travel. A deer's nose is its primary safety tool. So that they can scent danger over a wide expanse upwind of their position, deer most often angle across the prevailing wind. If the deer walks directly into the wind, it's unable to scent danger lurking ahead off to its left or right. I copy the deer's behavior in an attempt to follow the animal's path and locate sign. I determine my direction based upon the predominant wind direction for the area I'm hunting."

■■■

"Food sources are the primary key to patterning flatland deer. By tracking sign away from the food source, you will begin to identify patterns."

■■■

WALKING THE GRID

"If I've lost contact with sign that indicates deer activity and I'm not sure what's ahead, I walk a grid beginning at the area where I last spotted sign," Rohm adds. "Walking a grid allows me to systematically and efficiently cover a lot of ground as I look for more sign, a food source, bedding or watering area."

What Rohm means by walking a grid is traveling away from the starting point in a direct line, walking a set distance

Sky-High Scouting

Obtaining aerial photos of hunting properties used to be time-consuming and expensive. The Internet has changed all that. Although decent, and free, aerial images can be obtained from such sites as www.earth.google.com, high-quality photos can be obtained quickly and inexpensively from sites like www.terraserver.com. TerraServer offers possibly the largest variety of aerial photos, satellite images and USGS topographical maps on the Internet. The images and maps can be purchased as digital downloads or can be ordered as high-quality prints.

Even better options are available in some local areas that have their own county global information system Web site. Online GIS mapping access is usually free, or available for a nominal fee, and includes additional features, such as legal property descriptions, aerial maps with property boundary layers and the contact information for private landowners.

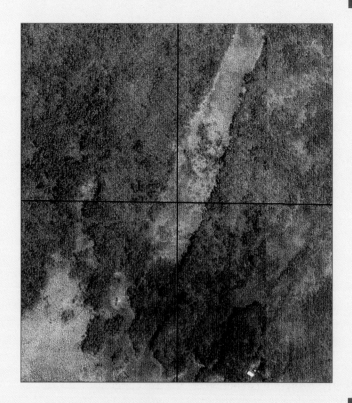

Hunting flat country — South and North alike — often involves hunting around water. The deer are used to it. You need to be able to deal with it.

then turning 90 degrees, moving 100 yards and turning again to travel a parallel path in the opposite direction. Rohm repeats the pattern, crisscrossing and scouting the entire area that he's interested in studying. As he travels, Rohm notes his observations on his topo map and saves key locations into his hand-held GPS. With locales saved in his GPS unit, getting back to an important site is simple no matter where he's positioned. Because Rohm always enters a region to hunt based upon the current wind direction, he might travel to the location from any compass point. Having a map, therefore, is crucial.

STAND ON THE FLATS

Beyond patterning the deer's movement, stand location and stand type are primary concerns when hunting flatlands. Because visibility from a treestand is minimal, usually about 100 yards, hunters must carefully choose a stand that will put them close to passing deer. In addition, in flatland regions, trees capable of holding a stand might not be available. Hunting from the ground is often a necessity.

■■■

"A hunter must pinpoint the exact tree that will see feeding activity and place his stand nearby."

■■■

"In rolling or mountainous terrain, seeing 400 to 500 yards isn't a problem," Rohm says. "From a bottom you can observe ridge faces in either direction. From a ridge, you can cover activity below as well as on adjacent ridge faces. Flatland stands don't offer that luxury. As a result, positioning a stand, tree or ground, so you can observe activity around five or six major oaks scattered across a wide area isn't possible.

"A hunter must pinpoint the exact tree that will see feeding activity and place his stand nearby. This is also the case when positioning stands along travel trails or at bedding sites. High-use areas must be identified. Rarely can these determinations be made weeks in advance of a hunt because regions frequented by deer change as weather conditions and food sources change and hunting pressure increases. That's why I like to scout while I'm hunting."

Rohm knows that the information that he gathers as he travels between stand sites can be used to his advantage a few days later. Identifying an oak loaded with acorns that haven't yet begun to drop, noticing signs of recent browsing activity or seeing a fresh bed or scrape near old sign tell Rohm a lot. The acorn tree soon to drop an abundance of food is worth traveling back to for an afternoon hunt a couple of days later. Fresh sign alone could have been made by an animal simply passing through the area. However, a combination of fresh and old sign indicates continued use by deer.

■■■

"A combination of fresh and old sign indicates continued use by deer."

■■■

BE FLEXIBLE

Rohm urges flatland hunters to move if a selected site is unproductive. Don't get hung up sitting in the same stand for more than a day or two if you're not seeing deer. The wandering nature of flatland deer is the reason for Rohm's suggestion. Although you worked hard to pattern the deer and pinpoint high-percentage hunting sites, a lack of action is reason to move. The deer might be close. You might have only missed the mark by 100 yards. Changing your luck often is as simple as changing your hunting site.

"Locating and identifying preferred food sources, becoming intimately familiar with the land and patterning deer activity are three critical keys to successfully hunting flatland bucks," Rohm says. "But that's not enough. Incorporating other whitetail hunting basics, such as eliminating human odor as much as possible, calling and rattling, using scents, and paying close attention to wind direction, is also a necessity. Outsmarting a white-tailed deer, whether it lives in the mountains of New York or the swamps of Mississippi, requires knowledge, skilled woodsmanship and the use of proven hunting tactics."

Don't sit and rot in one spot if nothing's happening: Get up and move your stand. Look for an area with both old and fresh sign.

Irresistible Grunts

C. J. WINAND

Many bucks — North, South, East and West — fall to deer calls each season.

Grunt calls have to rank right up there with treestands and compound bows as some of the most important pieces of modern deer hunting equipment.

Contrary to what you might have read from some of the so-called deer calling "experts," research has found that there are three different types of grunt vocalizations made by deer: tending, dominant and maternal. Since tending grunts are the ones most often heard by hunters, let's focus on them.

■■■

"What this means to hunters is that a series of three grunts is just as good as six or seven grunts in a row."

■■■

Biologists have found that these grunts average .72 seconds in length with no particular pattern nor sequence. What this means to hunters is that a series of three grunts is just as good as six or seven grunts in a row. In addition, researchers have found that just because a buck is old and big-bodied doesn't mean that he will have a low-pitched grunt. Just like human voices, some deer grunts are high and some are low. Still, hunters are advised to mimic a higher-tonality grunt call of a young buck.

Calling blindly can attract deer you might not otherwise have seen, but it also can educate deer you don't want to shoot (yearling bucks). Your best advice: Call when you see a shooter buck that's out of range and not likely to be heading your way. After you get its attention, put the call away and wait on the deer's reaction. Limit single grunts to about one second in duration.

Pressure-Cooked Whitetails

GARY CLANCY

Standing corn provides an incredible sanctuary for pressured bucks.

Back when I started hunting deer in the mid-1960s in my home state of Minnesota, the southern portion of the state had few deer. If you wanted to hunt whitetails (and about 500,000 Minnesotans did), you headed "Up North."

Up North was a wonderful semi-wilderness of 10,000 lakes, of course, but also plenty of whitetail habitat in the form of thousands of square miles of aspen, pine, spruce and maple forests interspersed with tamarack bogs, alder runs and clearcuts in various stages of regeneration. To a young man just getting started deer hunting, it was heaven.

But even back then, despite young legs and boundless energy, I found it impossible to leave other hunters behind. It's not that I'm antisocial, it's just that I prefer the company of other humans at ballgames, not in the deer woods. If, instead of spending so much energy trying to find solitude, I would have allowed other hunters to work in my favor and move deer toward me, success would have come to me much sooner.

The truth is, as much as we like to take credit for outsmarting a big buck, the majority of deer taken by deer hunters during firearms seasons die when they end up in your sights while trying to avoid being centered in someone else's. Anytime hunting pressure is sufficient to cause deer to disrupt their normal daily routine, it should automatically receive top billing when formulating a hunting plan. Although hunting pressure is heaviest during firearms seasons, I have seen a number of instances where bowhunting pressure was enough to cause deer to disrupt their daily travel patterns.

For years, I've been reading articles and book chapters that deal with hunting pressure. Invariably, the author will advise me to hike deeper into the timber than other hunters as a means of finding pockets of unpressured whitetails. Usually there will be some survey or study cited that claims to have discovered that 97.3 percent of all hunters never get more than 636 steps from their vehicles. I don't know where these studies were conducted, but I can tell you that in the places I hunt, enough hunters are willing to hike or ride ATVs deep into cover to make hunting pressure the overriding factor in my hunting strategy. Sure, hunter density decreases the farther you get from the last point of vehicle access, but solitude? Forget it.

Over the years I've learned a lot about how white-tailed deer, especially mature bucks, react to hunting pressure. When I began to use this information in combination with a plan of attack that features hunting pressure as the number one factor in determining how, when and where I hunt, my success rate on pressured bucks skyrocketed. You can enjoy the same success.

The only way to win in some cases is to keep the pressure on by wading right in.

LUNCHTIME IS PRIME TIME

Every deer hunter is pumped up and anxious at first light. We've been programmed to expect action during that first hour or two of the day. And there is no arguing the fact that natural deer movement is greatest at dawn and dusk. But when it comes to taking a mature buck when the pressure is on, the midday hours—from 10 a.m. until 2 p.m.—are well worth hunting.

It's during this period that many hunters take a few hours off from the hunt. Mature bucks take advantage of the quiet woods to stretch their legs, relieve themselves, grab a bite to eat, freshen a scrape or check a doe or two. Hunters patient enough to hunt all day are in position to take advantage of this midday movement.

Another advantage of all-day hunting is that you will already be in position to intercept deer that are disturbed by hunters vacating the woods at mid-morning and returning mid-afternoon.

However, few hunters can sit in one stand all day without becoming bored, and the bored hunter is a hunter who will fidget more than he should and pay less attention to his surroundings than he should. By moving my stand two or three times in a day to pre-scouted locations, I find that I can maintain the high degree of intensity that hunting for mature bucks demands.

Super Stands for Sneaky Bucks

Taking a stand and staying put while other hunters push deer past your position is the best way to take advantage of bucks under pressure. However, just walking into the woods, finding a comfortable tree to lean against and sitting down won't get the job done. Here are four specific stand locations that really produce anytime hunting pressure is a major factor.

1. RIDGE-RUNNER STANDS

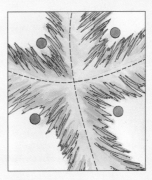

(Diagram A)

(Diagram B)

In hilly or mountainous terrain, mature bucks prefer to travel parallel to ridges and about one-third of the way down from the crest of the ridge. This information is nothing new to veteran hunters, many of whom have been hunting from stands located along that magical corridor for years.

But if you really want to up your odds on big bucks in hill country, take this concept a step further and look for those places where two or more ridges intersect (see Diagram A) or for those hard-to-find but dynamite locations where a series of ridges drop into a valley as in Diagram B.

Many veteran whitetail hunters believe that deer use particular landmarks like ridge intersections or a series of ridges descending into a valley as reference points in their travels. Fishermen call these types of underwater areas "structure." Abrupt changes in topography are always places to check out.

Continued on the next page.

Super Stands Continued . . .

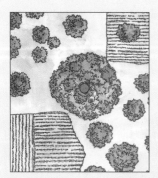

2. CLAUSTROPHOBIC STANDS

I hate hunting these stands. Cover so thick you can't see more than 30 yards. The whole time you just know that you should be sitting in those open hardwoods where you have a panoramic view for 100 yards or more. But then, with just the slightest whisper of brush sliding against slick hair, he's there.

Claustrophobic stands require an all-day commitment. Climb down and no matter how careful you are, the buck will hear you and either hold tight or slink away.

3. SADDLE UP

When a buck crosses from one side of a ridge to the other, he does so at select locations. Invariably, these locations are saddles, which are simply depressions in the ridge that allow the buck to slip over to the other side without exposing himself on the skyline. Don't get greedy and put the stand on the crest of the ridge so that you can cover both slopes and the saddle. The slightest movement will give your location away. Better to slip down one slope or the other and be able to cover the saddle and one trail.

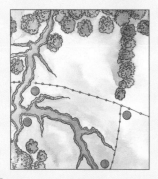

4. TRAVEL CORRIDORS

When a mature deer decides to put some distance between itself and hunters, it has a plan. Nine times out of 10 this route will include a series of travel corridors. A travel corridor is anything a deer can use to avoid detection while it travels from one location to another. The list is endless, but notables are fencelines, ditches, creekbottoms and windbreaks. The key locations are those where two or more of these travel corridors intersect.

LAST-MINUTE BUCKS

One thing you can count on when hunting whitetails in Canada in late November is cold weather. For 12 days I had toughed it out on stand, hoping for a crack at one of the big bucks this country has become famous for. Now, down to the last hours of my final day, all I had seen were does and a few small bucks. It would have been easy to give it up, climb down from the stand and get an early start on the long drive home.

The temperature that final day had been well below zero when I reached the stand just before first light. At noon, when I checked the small thermometer that I carry in my fanny pack, the mercury had not yet managed to nudge above the zero. I had seen only two does in the first hour of light and a small buck that came to the rattling horns at mid-morning. I kept reminding myself that three of my best whitetails have come during the

final minutes of shooting light. Pressure or no pressure, these are magical minutes, so I snuggled deeper into the pile-lined warmth of my Ravenwear coat and bibs, and waited.

My watch showed only seven minutes of legal shooting time left when I heard sticks breaking back in the jackpines and then the steady grunting of a buck chasing a doe. The sound faded and my heart sank, but then sticks crackled even closer. When the doe hotfooted it out of the dark pines and into the stand of popple where I waited, I just knew that the grunting buck behind her was a good one. When the heavy ten-point went down in a heap just 40 yards away, I glanced at my watch. One minute to go.

It amazes me how many hunters do not hunt these precious last minutes. Maybe they're cold, tired or bored. Perhaps they just want to get back to camp before dark. And many who do stick it out to the end tend to hunt stands closer to their vehicle

Hunting pressure comes in many forms. When push comes to shove, use hunting pressure to your advantage instead of trying to escape it.

or camp instead of sitting at prime locations. Big mistake, because big bucks have nocturnal tendencies anyway. Add the effects of hunting pressure, and some of the big guys just refuse to move until the woods are swallowed in evening's shadow.

HABITUAL HOMEBODIES

Like me, you probably believed that when things get hot and heavy, the mature bucks head for the hills and just keep on traveling until they find a place to hide until the season is over. But research involving free-ranging whitetails outfitted with radio transmitters has proven us wrong.

Even in the face of heavy hunting pressure, white-tailed deer are homebodies. Instead of heading for parts unknown, a mature deer learns to take advantage of all cover within its home area. These studies revealed that even when sanctuaries where no hunting was allowed were only a short distance away, deer did not take advantage of them during periods of intense hunting pressure unless the sanctuary was already part of the deer's home range.

Deer move more often when hunting pressure is a factor, but total movement, meaning the distance traveled during the period, did not increase significantly. What this means to us is that a whitetail under pressure will move only as far as it needs to in order to escape the immediate threat. And, as a deer matures, it will learn to remain still and let hunters pass it by.

In a Missouri study where both deer and hunters were monitored, hunters were often within 10 steps of bucks without knowing it. The mature whitetail is a master at using whatever

The author's Colorado buck proved that deer are often closer than we think.

Master of disguise. Sure, he's easy to see now. Wait 'til you're looking for him this fall.

cover is available to him. Combine this mastery with nerves of steel and you have one tough customer on your hands.

A CASE STUDY

One October I had the opportunity to hunt deer in southeastern Colorado. Both mule deer and whitetails call the sagebrush prairies and cottonwood creekbottoms home. On the morning after a freak blizzard blew through, leaving a foot of snow and cold in its wake, I was sneaking through a creekbottom when I spotted a mule deer doe standing about 100 yards away. Further inspection with my 10X50mm Swarovski binoculars revealed that the doe was not alone. Bedded beside her was a monster muley, a deer I immediately recognized as the buck the outfitter had named "Stickers" in honor of the dozen or so sticker points on the incredibly high and massive 4x4 frame. I slid down alongside a cottonwood, found the buck in my scope and slipped off the safety on the Browning Eclipse prototype rifle I was shooting. Just then, antlers moved on the big buck's hind end! I cranked the variable scope up to 10X and found a smaller buck, mostly covered with snow, lying directly behind. There was no way I could shoot without risking that the 165-grain .30-06 Winchester bullet would pass through the big buck and strike the smaller buck. I waited. These deer were relaxed, the wind was in my favor, and I knew that sooner or later the deer would get up out of their beds. When they did, I planned to be ready.

But I wasn't ready when the doe suddenly spooked at the sound of a distant truck, whirled and ran. The bucks sprang from their beds and followed the doe before I could get a clear shot. Still not believing what had just happened, I took up the track of the big buck. It was easy to follow. I trotted on the track as long as the buck was running, then slowed to a crawl when the tracks indicated that he was walking. For a half mile the trail took me down through the creekbottom where I lost the big buck's track in a maze of other deer tracks. As I crisscrossed the creekbottom, trying to unravel the buck's track from all of the others, I glanced up and saw a mule deer doe standing just 30 yards in front of me. The doe hadn't seen me, so I froze and just stood there as she fed slowly along.

Finally, after 20 minutes, the doe had moved far enough off to one side that I figured I could slip around her without spooking her. I took one step and a big white-tailed buck exploded from a small patch of thick willow-whips just ten steps to my left. I whirled, saw that the buck was a good one, and threw the Browning to my shoulder. The buck, a wide, heavy, long-tined eight-pointer was a mere 30 yards away and charging hard when I swung the crosshairs behind his right shoulder and touched the trigger. The buck went down in a billowing shower of snow.

Had it not been for the mule deer doe, I would have walked right past that buck. After admiring him, I backtracked the few steps to where the buck had been holding tight in the willows. There I found his bed marked with a perfect indentation of the buck's neck and chin. In an effort to make himself as invisible as possible, the buck had bellied into the willows with his neck and chin stretched out flat on the snow. Nerves of steel: This describes today's pressure-cooked whitetails.

Hunting the Nocturnal Buck

LARRY WEISHUHN

The moon was a thin, silver sliver in the dark November sky. And a brisk northerly wind made the night seem even colder. Legal shooting hours ended seven hours earlier in the day. I glanced over at my partner, Ron Porter, then a game warden with the New Mexico Department of Game & Fish. "Is it time?" he asked. I nodded, and we left camp and headed off into the darkness.

We were conducting a nighttime spotlight game survey and we hoped to observe some of the white-tailed bucks on one of the ranches I had under an intensive quality deer management program. The ranch also served as a white-tailed deer research area.

Earlier in the day, we advised a local Texas game warden of our plans for that evening and invited him to accompany us. Occasionally he did, but tonight he was busy elsewhere.

We spotted deer almost immediately upon setting out, but what really caught our eyes was the fact that these were different deer; different from those deer we'd been getting a look at during the day. Most notably, we saw several bucks that were some of the very largest specimens on the ranch, including four particular animals that I had caught only fleeting glimpses of during daylight hours. These bucks were night owls. I could observe them fairly regularly between the hours of 1:30 a.m. and 3:30 a.m. Outside of this timeframe, it was as though these bucks did not exist at all. Sure, I'd stumbled across a few of their shed antlers during the past few years. Yet, they still seemed ghostly. In fact, I was the only one who'd ever seen them at all.

As I mentioned, the ranch, approximately 1,000 acres in size, was intensively managed to produce big whitetails. It was surrounded by an eight-foot mesh wire fence, not so much to

■ ■ ■

"Outside of the nighttime, it was as though these bucks did not exist at all."

■ ■ ■

Every day the scrape's ripped to shreds, but you can't lay your eyes on him because he's a night prowler. How do you get him?

keep the deer in but to keep deer from neighboring properties out. Otherwise the management benefits to the deer on the property would have been greatly diminished. The deer inside the high fence had everything they needed and wanted to eat. We had taken care of the native habitat and offered supplemental feed available in troughs 24 hours a day throughout the year. We'd even planted and fertilized food plots around the property. These whitetails wanted for nothing!

■■■

"None of the hunters ever reported seeing any of the four bucks we gawked at that night. That did not surprise me."

■■■

Throughout the hunting season there were hunters in the field nearly every day. Each year we harvested a considerable number of does and a quota of bucks based on deer densities, fawn survival rates, buck-to-doe ratios and long-term management goals. The hunters were required to keep detailed records of does, fawns and bucks observed from each hunting stand. Information on bucks included number of points, spread, mass, and, if possible, a photo or video record was also included. None of the hunters ever reported seeing any of the four bucks Ron and I gawked at that night. That did not surprise me.

In my opinion, these particular deer could truly be classified as nocturnal bucks. And those four were not the only bucks on the ranch that adopted nocturnal behavior as they matured.

Another of our nocturnal bucks was one that had been bottle-raised by the ranch foreman and his wife, and for the first year of its life, it was a pet. When the buck turned 4 years old, the only time he was seen was after dark. He had large tags in his ears so he was plainly marked and should have been easy to identify. All of this makes me wonder how many totally nocturnal bucks there are in any deer population.

DOING IT ALL NOCTURNALLY

Deer tend to move for two reasons: hunger or breeding. Several of the totally nocturnal bucks I kept tabs on fed only at night, and they also tended to chase does only after dark. Is there a chink in the armor of these bucks, or are they the bucks that are simply unkillable?

In the case of the bucks inside the 1,000-acre enclosure, they were extremely familiar with their habitat. When hunters were on the ranch, the bucks rarely moved during daylight hours. And when they did, it was when the hunters were back at camp. Had I not shown the owner and his family the deer after dark, they likely would not have believed such huge bucks existed on the property.

He didn't get this big by showing off those antlers in daylight.

I mentioned deer "move" for one of two reasons. In the case of this particular ranch, the deer had plenty to eat. The food was available 24 hours per day, and they did not have to hustle to fill their rumens. They could eat a belly full in a matter of a few minutes, any time of the day or night. Unless the rut was going on, the breeding drive of the nocturnal bucks did not come into play. What I noticed, however, was that the nocturnal bucks on that ranch, and several other operations I have dealt with, tend to be at least five years old or older. They generally had extremely good antler development.

They also did not appear to be particularly sexually active. If a willing doe happened to enter the home area of one of these bucks, he might pursue her as long as she stayed in the thick brush. But if she left the safety of the cover in his core area, he would not follow. Regardless of the urges or circumstances, the urge to survive was stronger than anything else among those particular bucks.

I suspect that there are nocturnal bucks, such as those mentioned, throughout the whitetail's range. According to biologists, wardens, guides and outfitters and hunters I have talked to throughout the country, they tend to agree. In most every instance, nocturnal bucks tend to have huge antlers, generally among the best to be found in the respective areas.

HUNTING THESE CHALLENGING BUCKS

Are such bucks impossible to take? I think in some instances they might be. When most finally die, it is from natural causes or they meet their end by a vehicle on a highway in the wee hours of the morning. Or they are taken by a novice hunter who does not know that the unkillable nocturnal bucks cannot be taken. Perhaps therein lies the chink in the armor of the nocturnal super buck. Many of the biggest bucks are taken by rather inexperienced hunters or by those who had no prior knowledge of a buck of huge proportions in the area. The inexperienced hunter does not know that these bucks are supposed to live in only the worst of thickets or in areas farthest from civilization. Thus, these hunters spend time near major roadways or very close to camp. They don't try rattling or grunt calls and they don't confine their hunting efforts to those early-morning and late-afternoon hours that veteran hunters bank on.

What I'm trying to say is that we veteran deer hunters sometimes act more predictably than the whitetails. And it doesn't take a mature buck long to catch on to our tactics. After many years of dealing with big bucks, I have learned that deer tend to pattern hunters! Within the outdoor journals written about hunting whitetails it has become popular to pontificate about patterning whitetails. What most of these writers do not realize is that while they are patterning the deer, the deer, especially mature bucks, are patterning them! I have seen this happen many different times in a great variety of deer habitat.

■ ■ ■

"We veteran deer hunters sometimes act more predictably than the whitetails. And it doesn't take a mature buck long to catch on to our tactics. After many years of dealing with big bucks, I have learned that deer tend to pattern hunters!"

■ ■ ■

Your best odds of intercepting a nocturnal buck come on the edge of dark or at midday.

Want a buck like this? Don't settle for the status quo. Be different, hunt all day.

BE DIFFERENT

Matching wits with a monster whitetail is great fun and certainly a challenge. But do not out-think yourself, as a friend of mine who has taken numerous trophy bucks likes to say. According to him, there is a problem with falling into a rut when you hunt the nocturnal buck. You hunt the same general area day after day and use the same techniques as others. He advises to dare to be different. One of the best bucks he has taken came from what appeared to be an open field declared deerless by his fellow hunters. But right in the middle of the huge grassy field was a shallow depression, and unless you walked through the field you would never know it was there. My friend found it while on a mourning dove hunt. There he found several deer beds and one set of huge deer tracks. About three months later, he left camp four hours before daylight and found a comfortable place to wait in the middle of the depression. Just before first light, he heard a deer approach the area and bed down. When legal shooting light finally arrived, he shot a monstrous typical 12-point at 40 feet.

Back at camp, the landowner came by to look at the deer. According to him, he had seen the buck numerous times, but always at night when it crossed the road in front of his pickup. When I have seen nocturnal bucks during daylight hours, it has consistently been around the noon hour. Our hunters were in camp eating or resting, because they believed deer only moved early and late. Wrong! I have seen more big bucks during the middle of the day than at any other time. Deer that tend to move during the middle of the night also tend to move during the middle of the day. Knowing that one bit of deer behavior helped me take my biggest typical to date.

■■■

"Deer that tend to move during the middle of the night also tend to move during the middle of the day. Knowing that one bit of deer behavior helped me take my biggest typical to date."

■■■

That buck was taken at 11:35 a.m. after a night when the moon was full. If you want to take a nocturnal buck, be willing to hunt all day and hunt in areas that are avoided by others because they are "too open," "too close to camp," or "too close to a road." Find these unhunted pockets and you just might find the hiding place of the nocturnal buck.

Wait for Lunch-Bucket Bucks

LARRY WEISHUHN

You can't see this from your sofa at noon Sunday. Though it's unlikely you'll see a lot of midday deer, mature bucks are susceptible when you take your lunch bucket along.

Maybe most deer hunters just don't believe what they've been hearing for years. After all, it's difficult to imagine a trophy white-tailed buck up and about when the sun is high in the sky. Believe it.

Doubt keeps that same question coming. "What time of the day do you see the biggest bucks?" I was on stage at the North American Hunting Club Jamboree and had my answer ready when an NAHC member fired the query at me.

"I've seen more big bucks between the hours of 11 in the morning and 3 in the afternoon than during any other time of the day. This as a wildlife biologist and a serious whitetail hunter!" I replied.

Sometimes the question is phrased differently, "When's the best time to shoot a big buck?"

My response to this one at the Jamboree brought a wave of laughter. "Any time you see him during the legal hours of the hunting season!"

Big bucks traveling and vulnerable during midday hours just seems to fly in the face of what we've been taught as hunters. After all, we see more deer during early morning and late afternoon. But, while that might be true, the point of this discussion is mature bucks. And though you might see only one deer at 11 a.m. or noon, it might be the right one. Plus, how many of us are really out there putting in the hours from 10 a.m. to 3 p.m.? Not many.

THE COAST IS CLEAR

I don't know whether it's natural for deer to move during the middle of the day or whether the deer, especially mature bucks, have learned to adapt to typical hunting pressure. Most hunters are in the woods from just before daylight until about 9 a.m. and then again later in the afternoon. About the time hunters head to camp after a morning's hunt to share reports, have a bite to eat and watch the football game, the deer start moving. Then, at around 3 p.m. when hunters begin heading back to the deer woods, the deer sneak back to their beds. It makes sense.

Maybe deer have patterned hunters better than we've been able to pattern the deer! I have seen middle-of-the-day deer movement everywhere I've hunted whitetails, from just below the tundra in Canada to the cactus country of Mexico, and from the foothills of the Rockies to the swamps of the Carolinas. But the only reason I've witnessed this activity is because I've been in the field hunting during these times across the whitetail's range.

Deer are bedded more than afoot. But they will get up and move. That's why patience and all-day hunting pay.

I can't always spend all day in the field hunting, but whenever I have the chance, I do. If you're not hunting all day, you're missing opportunities to tag the biggest buck of your life.

Hunting pressure, as mentioned earlier, could be one of the forces leading to midday deer movement. Other theories revolve around moon position or climatic conditions. Even though this information doesn't determine whether or not I hunt, it probably does have an effect on when and why deer move. I hunt hard all day long, regardless of moon phase or position. For years, I have maintained a journal noting when I've seen deer and what they were doing while I observed them. In going through that journal, it strikes me that, throughout the fall, I have seen considerable deer movement during the middle of the day. But I've witnessed the most deer movement, regardless of sex and size of the deer, on those days following a full-moon night or a total dark-of-the-moon night.

THE MOON CONNECTION

Frequently, I hear hunters complain that when there is a full moon at night, deer feed and bucks chase does throughout the night and then bed down during the day. Admittedly, some scientific research indicates that this is the case. However, in my experience, when the moon is full all night long, most of the deer bed down. For years, I spent considerable nighttime hours with a light doing deer research on private property set up as a research area. My studies showed that when the moon was full and came up an hour or so after dark, there was con-

siderable deer movement during the last moments of daylight and the first hour of total darkness. Then, as soon as the moon rose, deer bedded and movements were substantially reduced. This pattern seems to hold true regardless of region.

On those nights when there was no moon, there was more movement than on full-moon nights, but not as much as on those nights when the moon was in different phases in between.

■ ■ ■

"Frequently, I hear hunters complain that when there is a full moon . . . bucks chase does throughout the night and then bed down during the day."

■ ■ ■

One of the ranches where I conducted nighttime research supported numerous huge bucks. The ranch received considerable hunting pressure primarily to remove does and bucks that did not measure up to our quality deer management standards. The property was hunted every day of the season, which lasted for approximately two months.

Most nights, I was up all night with a light, looking at and studying deer. I could regularly find the biggest bucks on the high-fenced 3,000-acre property, but only between the hours of 1 a.m. and 3 a.m. Our hunters never saw those bucks. I saw them only three times during daylight hours, between the hours of noon and 2:30 p.m. Each time, our hunters were back at camp.

Deer move primarily because of two factors during the fall: hunger and the rut. When they move depends upon weather conditions, food availability, hunting pressure, buck-to-doe ratios and other factors. But mature deer have a tendency to move during the middle of the day. I don't really know why that happens; I simply know that it does.

■■■

"Mature deer have a tendency to move during the middle of the day. I don't really know why that happens; I simply know that it does."

■■■

SUCCESS: A BIG DAYTIME BUCK

Several years ago I hunted some property in South Texas. Late one evening on our way back to camp in the dark, we spotted a huge eight-point buck as he crossed the road in front of us. He had long tines, good mass and was at least 23 inches wide. I hunted the deer the rest of the season without any success.

The following fall a ranch hand spotted a monstrous eight-point buck about three-fourths of a mile from where we had seen the big eight-point the previous year. Knowing I appreciated huge eight-points, he called to tell me about the buck and where he had seen him.

Late at night on January 1, I drove to the ranch. There was hardly need for headlights because the moon was so bright. The next morning I was up before daylight and spent some time hunting along the edge of a dry creek bottom. I rattled in several young bucks, but nothing that was really of interest. I knew the property held some huge bucks. About 10 a.m. I walked to my vehicle and drove back to camp to see if some of the others in our group had returned. When no one was in camp, I headed back to the brush. At approximately 11:45 a.m. I spotted several does feeding in a wide prickly pear flat. I watched them through my binoculars and caught movement behind the does and off to the right. Moments later a long-tined, massive buck appeared. I could see that he had eight points, but I did not know how wide he was. Still, it was apparent that I wasn't going to pass up an opportunity at a buck of this quality — if I got the chance. He slowly fed along, quartering toward the does.

I got really excited when he turned to look at something behind him. All racks look more impressive from the rear than from any other angle, but this one looked unbelievably wide! Hurriedly, I found a rest for my .309 JDJ Contender. When the crosshairs settled on the deer's shoulder, I squeezed the trigger.

I lost sight of the buck due to the recoil, but saw no sign of him running away. I reloaded and walked quickly toward where I had last seen the buck. Rounding a clump of cactus, I was confronted by the best deer I had taken up to that time. He had eight long points with one short kicker. He also had long main beams and was he ever wide! A quick look at my watch showed that it was 11:59 a.m.

Later that night, we gathered at camp and measured the buck's spread at 26 inches. Both main beams were 26 inches long, and the antlers scored 162 on the Boone and Crockett Club scoring system, if that's important to you. He was the best typical whitetail taken with a handgun by an NAHC member that year.

Did I ever tell you about this other deer I shot during the middle of the day in Iowa, and then there was the one in Michigan, and the one in Wyoming, and . . .

A midday buck might move only a short distance, but that might be just far enough. To see him, be out there hunting.

The Right Track

BRYCE TOWSLEY

If there is one certainty in modern deer hunting, it's that the whitetail boom has made us poorer hunters. As technology brings us more and more products for hunting and the strategies we use become more homogenized, we are slipping toward a generation of deer hunters who don't know a beech from a birch. As we hunters lose touch with the dynamics of the deer woods, we become merely interlopers — there only to shoot a deer — as opposed to predators who are an active part of the cycle.

Undeniably, the almost universal use of treestands and blinds has made us more effective at harvesting deer even though it's blunted our hunting skills. It's just not all that difficult to find a place with lots of fresh deer sign and to wait there for a deer to return. Simply put, we "modern" hunters are effectively "ambushing" deer. As a result, those valuable old woods skills of generations past have been mostly buried with old hunters.

THE ART OF TRACKING

Tracking is one of those hunting art forms that is nearly lost. On the surface, tracking can be viewed simply as locating a fresh deer track and following it until you see and shoot the deer. At its core, however, tracking will call on almost every hunting instinct available to man. Those of us with instincts dulled from a lack of time spent in wild places will struggle to read the sign correctly. Only a woodsman with a profound understanding of whitetail behavior will succeed. Luckily, we can be trained. We can even train ourselves. But you won't become an expert tracker by reading one magazine article. You will need to spend more time in the deer woods and look at deer hunting with a different eye.

Trackers see all of the whitetail's terrain instead of focusing on small areas around a stand. It's one on one, man following deer, and few disagree that it's also the most difficult way to hunt trophy bucks. Oddly, depending on the region and the conditions, tracking can also be the very best way to consistently take trophy bucks. That doesn't mean, however, that sloppy tracking technique will be forgiven even in the best situation.

Tracking is often considered regional and to some extent it is. Many northeastern deer hunters spend a good deal of time tailing whitetails. However, tracking works in any area with snow, whitetails and vast chunks of forest, field or prairie open to the hunter.

In these big-country wilderness areas, deer densities are usually low, and there are often miles of deer-less country between trophy bucks. As a result, bucks living in these regions are often vagabonds — wide-ranging animals that can cover a lot of turf, especially around the rut. Buck sign that was fresh yesterday could have been made by a deer that's now miles away with no intention of returning. Tracking is the most effective way to hunt that buck.

Tracking isn't for everyone. It is incredibly demanding, both physically and mentally. You must be able to walk for miles, all the while maintaining complete mental awareness. Often you will find yourself miles from camp or car when darkness falls, meaning more walking, and you must be able to get up and do it again the next day, the one after that, and for as many days as it takes. You need complete comfort in the woods without fear or even thoughts of getting lost, and when you finally shoot a buck, you might find yourself with a 250-pound deer and six miles of wilderness between you and the road.

It's work — heart-wrenching, back-breaking, discouraging work. But the hunters who do it (and they are an increasingly smaller percentage of today's hunters) say that there isn't a more effective way to kill a large, big-woods buck.

Tracking Packing

Tracking trophy bucks means you are going to be venturing into the deep woods at the time of year with the most unpredictable weather. Getting lost and spending the night in the woods carries with it the threat of hypothermia.

A modern GPS with an electronic compass can be extremely helpful, but it's also wise to carry a traditional compass, along with maps of your areas. Even in areas without service, carry your cell phone. If you get lost, turn it on anyway. The internal signal can sometimes still be traced by emergency crews. Be sure to bring extra batteries for everything, even equipment that runs on long-life lithium charges. You never know when you'll need them. Include a space blanket, some candy and granola bars and a small flashlight. You will need something to start a fire, so include a butane lighter and a magnesium fire starter. Never depend on just one source for starting a fire. A couple of candle stubs and some good tinder double-wrapped in plastic bags could be a lifesaver. Make sure that you also have a good knife and something to drag or carry your buck with.

Where It Works

It's probably fair to say that tracking has its largest number of practitioners in the extreme Northeast. While Vermont, New Hampshire and Maine are the primary focus for this kind of hunting, there is no doubt that it will work any place with vast expanses of land, big whitetails and snow during the hunting season. The northern forested regions of states like Minnesota, Wisconsin, Michigan's Upper Peninsula and Canada are also perfect. Another requirement is low hunter numbers; chasing the buck to another hunter is frustrating.

I hunted for whitetails in the extreme northwestern corner of Montana last fall and found that the vast expanses of national forest and relatively low deer densities were ideal for tracking. The Benoits have used their skills in Saskatchewan with good success, and I have tracked whitetails in Alberta, Saskatchewan and even Colorado. My friend Gary Merrill uses his tracking skills in New Brunswick with super results.

Some areas require a little adapting. In the farm country along the Battle River in Alberta, a buck can wander for miles along the huge agricultural fields. We actually used a four-wheel-drive truck to follow the track of one buck for nearly ten miles before isolating him in a large section of woods. I doubt that we would have caught up if we were walking all that time. Once we pinpointed the block of woods, we tracked on foot. I'd like to say that I got that deer, but he was simply better than I was that day.

Many of the Canadian provinces now have guide restrictions that don't allow a hunter to wander around on his own. So, before you send a deposit for an outfitted whitetail hunt, make sure you understand the law and the outfitter's policies.

THE RUT: PRIME TRACKING TIME

The rut plays an important role in this. A mature buck has only one thing on its mind during this time: finding does in heat and breeding them. He will travel endlessly in search of them. His single-mindedness will have him traveling more or less in a straight line from doe to doe. He might spend some time with a doe in estrus, but before long he's gone again.

He will eat very little and will bed only for a few hours at a time. This constant movement, coupled with the distraction of breeding, makes him easier to kill than at any other time of the year. Not easy . . . but easier! The first step is finding the lone track of a mature buck. Most hunters cruise logging roads slowly at first light, watching carefully for places where a big buck crossed during the night. In regions without this option you can do the same by walking trails, checking funnels and other likely travel locations.

READING THE SIGN

Because tracking is so demanding, only hunters after a trophy buck will make the sacrifice. So identifying the track as that of a trophy buck is important. Size is the best indicator. There are very few 275-pound does out there, and if the track is a real monster then you can be reasonably sure it is that of a buck, probably a trophy buck.

Of course, many mature bucks will have dressed weights of 200 pounds or less, depending on the region. A big-footed doe can leave a track as large, so you must look for other signals. Look at the pattern as well as the individual tracks. Like men and women, bucks and does are built differently. A trophy buck's stance is wider. He swaggers like a thick-chested football player when he walks. Does generally keep their feet in line in a more dainty manner. A big buck tends to drag his feet where a doe will pick hers up. These drag marks are evident in snow a few inches deep, but anything much deeper and all deer will show drag marks.

A buck might rub trees and make scrapes as he travels along and that is as sure a sign as you can hope to find. Also, a doe will travel through and under brush that a big buck has to go around to avoid tangling his antlers. Another clue is that a buck will urinate as he walks along, making dribble marks in the snow like an incontinent old fool. He might leave urine marks in the snow as much as five feet long; a doe usually will squat and go in one place.

Picture-perfect conditions. When you get a day like this, don't go to your treestand. It's time to lace up the walking boots.

Run 'n Guns

Whether it's a pump, autoloader or bolt, you'll want a familiar rifle that leaps to your shoulder and points like your finger.

If you're going to be walking ten miles a day up and down mountains, through swamps and across grown-over clear-cuts, you probably don't want to be lugging a ten-pound magnum rifle. But while weight is a consideration, "shootability" is perhaps a more important one. Most times you will need to shoot quickly. Having a gun that fits you and that you have confidence in is the most important factor. If that gun is also light in weight, well, so much the better.

Many northeastern hunters favor Remington pump-action rifles. No doubt the fact that the Benoit family uses them is a big factor, as the influence of the Benoits on a generation of hunters is seen throughout the northeastern woods. I, too, can trace my love of these rifles to Larry Benoit. Long before I ever met the man, I bought my .30-06 Model 760 mostly because he used one. It wasn't until hunting with it that I discovered how right he was.

These days I have some of the finest rifles on the market in my gun room, but when I am hunting the thick woods of home, it's that worn old 760 that travels with me into the gray cold of a November dawn. Why? Because it fits me, and I shoot it well. There are, of course, many guns on the market that make excellent tracking rifles, including many lightweight models introduced in recent years.

Keep in mind that you are after some of the biggest whitetails on earth and the shots might not always be perfectly broadside, so pick a caliber that has a margin of extra power. The .270 Win. and the .30-06 are big favorites. Use medium to heavy bullets for the caliber to ensure penetration on an angling shot. These days I like the .35 Whelen in a 7600 pump with handloaded Barnes 200- or 225-grain X-Bullets. (Federal's 225-grain Trophy Bonded bullet should also work great in the Whelen.) The Benoits use peep sights, because they weigh less and are less troublesome than a scope. But peeps aren't for everybody. I have Leupold 1.5-5X Vari-X III scopes on both my Remington pumps, and I wouldn't switch. Again, they fit me well.

Look at where a buck has put his nose into another deer's track or lowered his head to grab a bite. If you see marks made in the snow by his rack, you can often make a judgment on his size in addition to being sure that it's a buck's trail you're on.

The best plan when tracking a deer is to catch him on his feet and walking away from you, usually traveling into or across the wind, trying to grab a whiff of a doe in heat. In these circumstances, he is vulnerable.

Of course, like people, every deer is different and each will act differently. That's where a woodsman earns his keep. An experienced tracker can read the deer and predict his movements. For example, if the deer is meandering and munching here and there, he might be getting ready to bed. The inexperienced tracker who misses this sign and keeps charging ahead is sure to spook the buck. A veteran tracker recognizes it and slows down. He hunts carefully and slowly, picking the woods apart with his eyes. He moves only after seeing everything within his range of vision. If he is good enough to see the deer before it sees him, the game is over; if not, it begins again.

If memory serves me right, it was Bill Jordan (the Texas Ranger and gun writer) who said about gunfighting, "Take your time, FAST!" The same might apply to tracking a deer. The biggest single reason that most hunters fail to see the deer they are tracking is that they do not move fast enough. The buck might have a several-hour start on you; if you pussyfoot around you will never catch up. The hunter needs to be able to cover ground fast when it's called for. At the same time, he needs to be quiet and alert so that he sees the buck before the buck sees him. That's the art of tracking, and many never master it.

You need a lot of land and a healthy dose of persistence to make tracking pay off.

BENOITS: TRACKERS EXTRAORDINAIRE

Some hunters have learned to unravel deer tracks with uncanny consistency. Take the Benoit family of northern Vermont. Larry Benoit likely became the first deer hunting celebrity when he burst onto the scene in 1970. We first saw him on a magazine cover along with a headline, "Larry Benoit — is he the best deer hunter in America?" Many who read his book and the many magazine articles that followed concluded that he was.

"You must be able to tell from the tracks when it is time to sling your rifle on your back and cover ground as fast as you can and when it's time to slow down and be careful," Larry says. The most critical time: those final minutes of the hunt. That's when most hunters get impatient and blow it. This is the point when you know you are close to the buck and everything depends on the next few moves. It's the most dangerous time in any hunt; when the senses of both the hunter and the hunted are tuned to their finest. The right step, the right pause; each decision impacts the outcome. And the buck has all the aces and wins most of the time.

The Benoits call it the "death creep," not so much for the expected demise of the buck, but because the hunter must move so slowly that he doesn't appear to be moving at all. Recently Shane and Larry Benoit were describing to me the necessity of maintaining complete focus.

"Your thoughts must be only and totally on the task at hand," one of them said. "You must think of nothing else but seeing that buck before he knows you are there." They explained how you must draw yourself into a state of total concentration.

"How do you maintain this, particularly when it must continue sometimes for hours?" I asked.

"How can I not?" replied Larry. "There is nothing I love more in life than hunting big white-tailed bucks. Maintaining the drive and the focus for deer hunting is as easy for me as breathing." Without similar drive and focus you are wasting your time tracking giant bucks.

If we could custom-order a day to track deer, it would have a fresh snow of about five inches. The temperature would be just above freezing, making the snow a soft and slightly wet cushion under our feet (in addition to muffling sounds, this soft snow shows a track very well). The trees and bushes would be bent under the new snow and, on the very best days, a soft, big-flaked snow would continue to fall.

Hemingway wrote about weather such as this and how it makes the animals easy to approach. Perhaps the falling snow and the changed landscape confuse the deer, who knows? But it's a day to track, and that's what the smart hunter is doing. If you find a big track early in the morning and you are good, that deer should be yours before dark. Move fast and silent on the track and try hard to kill the buck the first time you catch up to him. After that, he knows you are on his trail and things become more difficult.

But when your deer is down and you are sitting quietly, experiencing the unexplainable emotions that come when a tough hunt is over, you are certain to reflect on tracking and its difficulties. You remember the ordeal that brought you to this point, and you will think of the long drag out that you are faced with. You'll wonder if it is worth it.

Then you'll look at what is most likely the biggest buck of your life and you know the answer, because this is a deer that you have truly hunted and truly earned.

Vermont's Larry Benoit has come to depend on tracking as his favored method for tagging old northern bucks. With years of experience, the Benoits get on a track and expect success.

Hunting the Second Season

RICHARD P. SMITH

Hunting late-season whitetails with muzzleloader or bow can be cold and frustrating. Some of the coldest weather of the year commonly occurs during late deer seasons nationwide. Most times and most places, that makes it difficult to stay comfortable while hunting.

The effects of earlier hunts on deer can add to the challenge because numerous whitetails have already been removed from the population and those that are left are at their wariest. The surviving bucks are those most adept at avoiding hunters. However, if you go about it right, late-season hunting can also be the most rewarding. Trophy bucks are taken every year during these hunts and in some cases those animals are the largest whitetails ever tagged by hunters.

A MICHIGAN GIANT

That's certainly true for Michigan bowhunter Jerry Pennington, who bagged his best buck, a December monster. The typical 10-pointer qualified for a place in the Boone and Crockett Club and Pope and Young Club records. An unusual set of circumstances contributed to Pennington's success on his trophy buck during the state's late bow season. It might work in your favor sometime.

Wet weather that fall prevented farmers from harvesting an estimated 65 percent of corn crops statewide. The area that Pennington hunts had a lot of standing corn during December and that's where the deer were. Three rows of an 80-acre cornfield

He's still out there. But he's a veteran of many hunting days and, therefore, a harder animal to put in your sights.

Bows and muzzleloaders make late-season hunts even more challenging and rewarding.

were cut on December 21, and Pennington set up on the ground at the end of a peninsula of tall grass and weeds that extended into the field. The grass and weeds were high enough to conceal him while seated on a stool. It was cold and windy that evening, and Pennington didn't see a deer, but he was sure that the biting wind curtailed deer activity. So the next day he was back in the same place.

■■■

"All types of agricultural fields with food remaining will attract whitetails during late seasons. So will remnants of fruit and mast crops such as apples, acorns and beechnuts."

■■■

It didn't take long for whitetails to start appearing in the swath of corn that had been cut. A number of deer were busily feeding when the book buck finally appeared and walked by Jerry's hiding spot no more than 10 yards away.

Standing corn that remains during late season is always a whitetail magnet. Hunting along the edges of those fields as Pennington did is an excellent strategy when deer are bedding in the field. In situations where whitetails are bedding elsewhere, planning an ambush along their approach trail is best. If deer aren't reaching fields until after legal shooting time, try to set up as close to bedding areas as possible.

Gene Lengsfeld was only about 100 yards from farm fields planted with corn and alfalfa on December 7 when he bagged one of Minnesota's highest-scoring typicals. The exceptional 13-pointer that scored 182⅛ appeared well before dark, at about 3:30 p.m.

THE CROP CONNECTION

Hunters who prefer still-hunting or stalking can sometimes connect by sneaking through standing corn on windy days. Based on Pennington's lack of deer sightings the evening before he got his big buck, still-hunting rather than posting might be the best option when the wind is blowing hard enough to rattle corn stalks. Driving cornfields is another option, especially during muzzleloader seasons.

Although standing corn offers super late-season hunting opportunities, the same applies to any quality food supply that's available in your area. All types of agricultural fields with food remaining will attract whitetails during late seasons. So will remnants of fruit and mast crops such as apples, acorns and beechnuts. Oak trees of one type or another are found over most of North America, and whitetails always concentrate where the nuts are abundant. Many southern states have a variety of oaks, and it's not unusual for a number of species to produce nuts at the same time. Acorns from trees that are

members of the white oak family are usually eaten before those from red oaks. Deer often bed in the nearest heavy cover and make daily trips to stands of mast-producing hardwood trees, so plan an ambush along major trails between bedding and feeding areas.

LEVERAGE LOGGING ACTIVITIES

Logging operations where hardwood and evergreen trees are being felled can also be late-season hotspots. Whitetails love to browse on these trees. Some of my best late-season hunting has been at or near cuttings. One of my better blackpowder bucks was ambushed one December along a major trail leading to a cutting. The 11-pointer showed up late in the evening trailing a pair of antlerless deer.

Food, food, food. The way to a buck now is through his stomach.

SELECTING STAND SITES

For morning hunts, select stand sites near bedding areas that deer are expected to return to after feeding all night. One December morning, I collected a spike buck with a muzzleloader by posting near a bedding area where a bowhunting friend of mine had seen ten- and six-point bucks a day or two before. When the bigger bucks didn't show up, I took the spike because it was the last day of the season.

Although it's always nice to take a buck with a big rack, any whitetail taken during the late season can be considered a trophy. Late seasons are an excellent time to take antlerless deer, where legal. I've taken does during many seasons when time was running out and I had not yet seen a buck.

■■■

"The fact that hunting pressure normally drops off during late seasons can work in favor of hunters who take advantage."

■■■

CONSIDER BAITING AND BREEDING ACTIVITY

One last late-season tactic that can pay off, where it is legal, is baiting. Corn, apples and other types of foods that whitetails prefer can help lure them into position for a shot. Although this technique can increase the number of deer that late-season hunters are able to see, the method is often overrated in terms of its effectiveness. Antlered bucks frequently shun bait sites until after dark. Baits established on the edge of heavy cover or in cover where whitetails feel comfortable during daylight hours will be most effective during late seasons.

Although most breeding is over by the time late seasons begin, there might still be some does that haven't been bred, especially late-maturing, young does that will be breeding for the first time. If you see any fresh scrapes or rubs, that might be a sign of current breeding activity, and hunting nearby could produce action. There is usually lots of competition among bucks that are still alive to breed does that come into heat during late seasons.

It's mentally taxing and a physical battle to deal with late-season elements.

JUST GO HUNTING

The fact that hunting pressure normally drops off during late seasons can work in favor of hunters who take advantage. Whitetails often return to normal activities after hunting pressure declines. It might also be easier to get permission to hunt private property when competition for hunting spots is reduced. Farmers who have been experiencing crop damage from deer are often willing to grant permission to hunt. The same can be true of landowners who have suffered damage to gardens or ornamental plants.

Sure, late-season hunting can be difficult. But it can also provide you with some of the greatest challenges and rewards of the year. I can think of no better Christmas present than a late-December white-tailed buck.

CHAPTER 4

Hunting the Rut

You'd think it would be easy to explain what makes this part of the deer season so special. "Action" might be the best word. The whitetail rut is like hitting the flight of Northern mallards just right. It's like landing smack dab in the middle of a monstrous caribou migration. It's a wild spectacle.

At least it has the potential to be. That's because the rut, like migrations and other wildlife phenomena, is always shrouded by some mystery and uncertainty. Even now. Even during what should be the peak two-week period to be in the deer woods, when giant bucks should be thinking breeding first and survival second, when the time of the day is of little consequence, when we can still wait at a killer stand and see . . . nothing.

And the next day, the biggest buck you've ever seen slinks into the clear at 20 steps. That's how it goes. It's wildly unpredictable, and maybe that's what makes it so antler-clashing exciting. Every doe sighting leads to expectations of a trailing buck. Every rattling sequence or note on the grunt call could bring a bristling buck on a string. If you have one week of vacation to dedicate to deer, it would be difficult to justify timing it for any part of the season other than the rut.

From there all you can do is hope. Hope that on a cool morning an old whitetail is scent-checking his turf; maybe he catches a whiff of the doe-in-heat scent trail you put down under the cover of darkness. And maybe you get to see one of God's most incredible creatures up close.

Maybe . . .

■ ■ ■

When the Chase Is On

CHARLES J. ALSHEIMER

White-tailed deer hunters really need to start speaking the same language. In some regions of the U.S., the bare dirt found under a licking branch is called a "paw bed" instead of a scrape. Many hunters continue to incorrectly use the term still-hunting when referring to sitting motionless in a blind or treestand.

But of all the words and terms associated with deer hunting, the word "rut" is perhaps the most misused. To many hunters, the word refers to all whitetail scraping, rubbing, chasing and breeding activity that occurs during the autumn months. Though this might be the way hunters and writers look at the term, biologists refer to the rut as that period when the actual breeding takes place.

Based on this scientific definition, the rut is not the best time to hunt white-tailed bucks, especially mature bucks. As a matter of fact, the rut can be the most difficult and frustrating time to hunt deer because during this time the doe controls everything. Therefore, if you happen to be lucky enough to have an estrous doe near your stand, you'll probably see plenty of activity as bucks will be nearby looking for a piece of the action. No does, no bucks. And frustrating hunting.

Because of this, the whitetail's "chase phase" is the time that I concentrate my efforts for mature bucks. In scientific terms, the chase phase begins around October 15 in the northern half

■ ■ ■

"The whitetail's 'chase phase' is the time that I concentrate my efforts for mature bucks."

■ ■ ■

He'll dog her until he corners her and she'll stand. And as he chases, he's vulnerable.

Decoys are a fine idea during the chase phase, but it doesn't always end like this.

of the U.S., increases dramatically until it peaks during the first week in November, then begins to drop off as does come into estrus. It's during this time that bucks truly go bonkers and are most vulnerable.

In western New York, where I live, the most active time of the chase phase is from about October 25 to November 10. During this 17-day period, bucks are overdosed on hormones. However, the majority of does are not quite ready to breed. As a result, rubbing, scraping, fighting and chasing are at their peak as bucks frantically try to find a hot doe. Though New York's dates are only representative of the states north of the Mason-Dixon Line (Pennsylvania/Maryland border), the chase phase is consistently the three-week period prior to the peak of the breeding. So if you know when the peak breeding time is, the chase phase can be easily determined.

■■■

"The chase phase is consistently the three-week period prior to the peak of the breeding. So, if you know when the peak breeding time is, the chase phase can be easily determined."

■■■

Over the years, I've refined my hunting strategies to coincide with this time and have developed some definite do's and don'ts. Things happen rapidly during the autumn months as the rut approaches. For this reason, trying to hunt the chase phase like the pre-rut or early season will not normally work well. The key to hunting the chase phase is to react quickly to what's happening. You must be versatile and willing to experiment with new tactics.

CHASE PHASE DON'TS

A popular and effective approach for early season buck hunting is to set up near food sources and locations where bachelor groups have been sighted. When the chase phase kicks in, however, bachelor groups break up and bucks curtail their feeding habits. In some cases, they'll nearly quit eating as their system becomes overwhelmed with the urge to breed. As a result, I usually don't hunt food sources during the chase phase.

I know what you're thinking. The does are still feeding, and if the bucks are seeking out the does, food sources should be high-percentage spots. I disagree for two reasons. By this time of the season, most deer have been exposed to some hunting pressure and will concentrate their feeding during nighttime hours. Secondly, even when deer do hit food sources during the day, there is usually more than one set of eyes to contend with. Drawing a bow and making a good shot on a buck under

When you scout in autumn, keep disturbance to a minimum. Get in, make a plan, and get out.

deer's bedroom must be avoided. That means I try to do my major scouting in the winter months. Whitetails are creatures of habit, so travel corridors, scraping areas and bedding areas usually do not change drastically from year to year. Do your homework ahead of time by scouting in the winter and keep fall scouting to a minimum . . . this is critical.

Because of erratic deer movements, I seldom use permanent treestands, especially if they are built after leaves fall from the trees. Whitetails, mature bucks in particular, know their territory intimately and will shy away from the sudden emergence of a glob of wood 15 feet above the ground. Portable climbers and hang-on stands will allow you the mobility you'll need to stay a step ahead of the bucks.

■■■

"Try to hunt an area that has several nice bucks and take what the land gives you."

■■■

There's a lot of discussion today about patterning and hunting a particular deer. This talk is great for someone who is able to hunt the entire season and has access to large tracts of land. But less than 1 percent of America's deer hunters fall into this category. During the chase phase, a white-tailed buck's territory can be anywhere from 600 to 5,000 acres. There's no telling where he'll be on a given day. For this reason, I discourage the average weekend deer hunter from trying to hunt a particular buck. Doing so will mean an empty freezer and empty wall where you imagined that beautiful head mount. Instead, try to hunt an area that has several nice bucks and take what the land gives you.

CHASE PHASE DO'S

Once a whitetail's autumn behavior is known, a variety of techniques can be used to outsmart him. During the chase phase rubbing, scraping and doe chasing will be at a fever pitch. Though I love to hunt all seasons, my scouting is done with the chase phase in mind. During the winter months, I'm aggressively looking for food sources, funnels, old scrapes, rubs and bedding areas.

Whitetail bucks will use a scrape year-round, regardless of whether they have antlers or not. They use the scrape's licking branch to let other deer in an area know that they are around. In the process, they also leave an indication of their size. When a buck works the licking branch he always leaves a hoof print in the bare dirt. If the hoof print is wider than 2½ inches, it's a good bet that the deer weighs more than 175 pounds. Body size and antler size don't always go hand in hand, but it's a good start.

Crucial to chase phase success is hunting where the does are. From the time bucks disperse from their bachelor groups, they are searching for does. So, don't get discouraged if you're

these conditions is tough. One exception I've found is overgrown apple orchards and mast-producing trees located in very thick cover. Here does continue to feed during the day, and bucks will be close by. With thick cover to camouflage my movements, I feel very comfortable and confident hunting these areas during any of the fall months.

Scouting plays a major role in ambushing a nice buck during the chase phase. However, scouting must be kept to a minimum during the autumn months. Nothing will turn a white-tailed buck nocturnal faster than humans invading his territory, especially his bedding area. If you expect success, a

■■■

"Do your homework ahead of time by scouting in the winter and keep fall scouting to a minimum . . . this is critical."

■■■

During the chase phase, set up on a travel corridor where a doe will lead a buck right into your lap.

■ ■ ■

"Don't get discouraged if you're seeing a lot of does earlier in the season. Stay with them, and when the chase phase kicks in, you'll be in position for some great action."

■ ■ ■

seeing a lot of does earlier in the season. Stay with them, and when the chase phase kicks in, you'll be in position for some great action.

As I mentioned earlier, I usually don't hunt in the middle of food sources during the chase phase. Rather, I'll set up along frequently used travel corridors, between bedding and feeding areas where ample cover, scrapes and rubs are present. Every decent piece of whitetail habitat will have a place like this. Work hard to find it. These funnels might be thin necks of woods that connect various types of habitat. Maybe it's at a stream crossing. The key is that it provides ample cover and the security that deer are looking for.

Where to hang a stand between the bedding and feeding area can be a critical decision. Mature bucks tend to "scent-check" scraping locations. That means that they'll try to approach from downwind and let their nose determine whether or not to go all the way to the scrape. That being the case, I shy away from putting stands within 15 yards of a scrape. During bow season, I hang a portable stand 15 to 20 feet high, 25 to 60 yards downwind from the scrape, if the terrain permits. Dur-

ing the shotgun or rifle season, you can extend that distance out to 100 or more yards.

From there, scents and calls can be the ticket to luring a mature buck into shooting range.

In mid-October, when bucks begin dispersing, scrapes will begin to show up in the travel corridors. If a scrape appears in the same general area as the previous year, I begin to doctor the scrape with a good quality lure. You can do this by hanging a scent dispenser just out of a buck's reach on the licking branch. Try to set up three locations like this and keep them fresh with scent throughout the season. This technique works much the same way a scent post works for a fox trapper. It keeps bucks interested in the area.

By the time late October arrives, I'm laying down a scent trail every time I go to my stand. This is done by putting lure on the bottom of my boots when I'm within 100 yards of my stand. Make a trail where you'd like the deer to walk. Generally, I add lure to the boot bottoms every 30 yards until I'm about

■ ■ ■

"During bow season, I hang a portable stand 15 to 20 feet high, 25 to 60 yards downwind from the scrape, if the terrain permits. During the shotgun or rifle season, you can extend that distance out to 100 or more yards."

■ ■ ■

75 yards past my stand. Then I'll retrace my tracks, climb into the stand and get ready. Over the years, this technique has produced some very nice bucks.

One of the beauties of the chase phase is that bucks stay active most of the day. They bed very little. A whitetail has four active periods each day: generally dawn, midday, dusk and sometime during the night. During the chase phase these periods last longer. Therefore, try to hunt as many hours as possible during this magic time.

MORE DO'S: DECOY TECHNIQUES

Decoying whitetails is tailor-made for the chase-phase period. By setting up a buck or doe decoy in an area where deer can see it, a hunter can increase his chances of taking a nice buck. The beauty of decoying is that the deer's attention is on the decoy and not on the hunter. If a doe decoy is used during bow season, it works best when set up 20 to 25 yards in front of your stand. Position the decoy so you are looking at its rump as a buck will almost always approach it from the rear. If a buck decoy is used, have the decoy facing or angling toward you because bucks usually approach a buck decoy from the front.

If you would like to use a decoy, remember three things. First, to keep a buck's interest, try adding a little movement to the decoy. Lightweight white material attached to the ears or tail will help. To kill any human odor, thoroughly spray the decoy with a good scent destroyer after setting it in place. Also, you might try a doe-in-heat scent on the decoy's rump. Secondly, decoys are no guarantee for success. Every buck has a different personality, and all react differently to a decoy. About 30 percent of the time, a buck will spook or become alarmed when he encounters it. Finally, using decoys can be dangerous — especially during firearms seasons. Check local laws before using, be careful, wear blaze orange and use common sense.

FINAL DO'S: CALLING AND RATTLING

Probably one of the most exciting ways to hunt chase-phase whitetails is by calling them with antlers or grunt tubes. Calling works especially well when hunting over scrapes and using a decoy. The key is to know how and when to do it.

Factors like buck-to-doe ratios, number of mature bucks in the area and time of the season affect calling success.

Regardless of where you hunt, rattling and calling will work, though it will be better where there is a good age structure and buck-to-doe ratio.

My best rattling success has come when I rattle aggressively in thick cover. The key is to make your sequence sound like a full-blown buck fight. I've photographed many buck fights over the years, and only one lasted longer than five minutes. My rattling sequence consists of three 1½-minute rattling sessions, with a 30-second break between each session. If I'm hunting from a treestand, I'll rattle once every hour to try and lure any buck cruising through the area.

∎∎∎

"Calling works especially well when hunting over scrapes and using a decoy. The key is to know how and when to do it."

∎∎∎

But as good as rattling can be, using a grunt tube is my bread-and-butter strategy when hunting rut-crazed bucks. Scientists have identified many different whitetail vocalizations, but the doe bleat and the guttural grunt are the two calls I rely heavily on.

If I see a buck walking through the woods and realize that he will not come to me naturally, I'll try stopping him with a low guttural grunt. If he does not stop, I'll grunt louder. If he stops, I'll grunt again so he can pinpoint the sound and, hopefully, head toward me. As soon as he starts toward me, I'll shut up and let him try to find me.

The doe bleat is a call I use with a doe decoy or when the action is slow. If I see a buck and he does not see the decoy, I'll try two or three doe bleats — just enough for him to see the decoy and start toward it. If I'm not seeing deer, I'll use a doe bleat or buck grunt every 45 minutes or so. Sometimes this is enough to bring in a deer that otherwise wouldn't have shown itself.

The chase phase is by far the most exciting time to be in the deer woods, whether in Maine, Saskatchewan or Texas. The sound of antlers clashing and bucks grunting as they chase does through the woods are what deer hunting dreams are made of.

Get a Buck Out of the Rut

BY LARRY WEISHUHN

The rut doesn't always hit when we expect. What do you do when your hunting time and the rut fail to coincide?

"**T**hey running yet?" seemed to be the question of the hour as I pulled into the small South Texas town of Crystal City. People had come from distant states and gathered for a much anticipated annual event. And no matter what type of accent the foreigners spoke with, the query was the same. Right now, in Crystal City, everyone wondered if the South Texas whitetail rut was underway. I suppose the scene wasn't a whole lot different there than anywhere else hunters gather in anticipation of exciting deer hunting action.

The whitetail breeding season, or "rut," is actually determined by a decrease in daylight, regardless of whether the temperature is hot or cold. And its onset is determined by the does in the area, not the bucks. The bucks are practically ready for the breeding season to begin the same day the velvet comes off of their antlers. By then their testosterone level is greatly increasing and they are producing viable sperm.

RUT FACTORS

The rut generally is such that the breeding takes place so that the fawns are born 7½ months later. This timing is naturally in-
tended to put fawns on the ground during the most opportune time in respect to spring's increased food supply and quality of vegetation. That's why it's important that diminishing daylight is the factor that determines when does are ready to breed. But there are other external factors that can alter rut dates.

The physical health of the does in the local deer population can play a role in delaying the rut or altering its intensity. If does are emaciated, the rut might be a few days late. It can also be delayed if there was an extremely high fawn survival rate and the does are just now weaning fawns (as can happen in

■■■

"What do you do if it seems that there is no rut even if the time is right? The answer is simple. You return to the basics and hunt hard and long!"

■■■

some areas where there normally is a late fawning date). And sometimes it seems that there are other factors that come into play. I have often jokingly blamed sunspot activity, for a lack of a better definitive explanation.

Lower temperatures are generally associated with an increase in daytime deer activity, especially in terms of the rut. And while the cold weather might not have all that much to do with the timing of the rut, it seems to greatly increase deer activity. Part of the reason is that when deer go into the fall and winter, they grow a thick coat of hair to stay warm. When the temperature rises after deer have grown winter hair, deer sometimes become lazy and a bit sluggish, just as you might if

Even though whitetail hunters bank heavily on the rut, rattling often works best before and after the breeding season.

you were wearing a heavy wool coat every day regardless of the temperature. Now imagine this: After several days of above-normal temps, suddenly the temperature cools. Wouldn't you feel better since you no longer were suffering from the heat? Deer activity sometimes works the same way.

Interestingly, the rut occurs at essentially the same time each year, give or take a week, regardless of the weather. But when it is unseasonably hot, chasing and breeding activity takes place under the cool cover of darkness. And even though it might seem that there is no rutting activity going on, there is!

If that happens during the time you have planned to hunt, or you have made long-term vacation plans or traveled great distances, what do you do if it seems that there is no rut even if the time is right? The answer is simple. You return to the basics and hunt hard and long!

WHEN THE RUT IS NOT

When it seems that the rut has been delayed or deer activity is diminished in an area that you know holds a good deer population, return to hunting food sources. If you have done your homework, you will know the key whitetail forage plants for your specific hunting area during the different seasons. Return to those and hunt along the edges of thickets bordering these choice browse items. Many areas are set up ideally to hunt natural funnels leading from bedding areas to food sources. If you hunt areas that have rolling hills or abundant drainages, set a stand about a third of the way from the top, along trails that show heavy use by deer. Along these trails is also where you generally find both rubs and scrapes.

When the rut does not seem to kick in like it should, that does not mean bucks will no longer work scrapes. So don't totally abandon this tactic. Just make sure that you use care to set up downwind from an active scrape or scrape line. This is

---

Bend Branches for Scrapes

Pen studies have revealed that some bucks are prolific scrapers while others do not scrape at all. The same holds true for buck rubbing activity.

If you are hunting an area where your scouting does not reveal many scrapes, it might be due to a lack of an adequate supply of overhanging branches at the preferred height for scraping bucks. This can be especially true in habitat that has been heavily browsed by an over-populated deer herd. Deer researchers theorize that since there are hardly any overhanging branches for bucks to mark with their scent, the deer will not waste the energy to make a scrape. So what is a hunter to do?

Biologists have found that you can create suitable overhanging branches on or near deer trails, and that bucks will sometimes use such locations for scraping. Simply bend and tie a branch three to five feet above the ground, and there is a fair chance that a buck will scrape there if it is in a location where there is a severe lack of overhanging branches.

Another biologist and I tried this in such a region and found that within one week, 50 percent of our artificially tied-over branches had scrapes under them. We did not use any types of scent in conjunction with the overhanging branches, nor did we disturb the leaves on the forest floor below the branch.

— C.J. Winand

Does lead many bucks to their demise.

the pre-rut or chase period. Grunting and rattling can work great during these days. When there are a lot of does in heat at the same time, bucks seldom can be lured into a fight. They'd rather tend to the does. Before and after breeding, however, rattling and grunting are effective techniques.

Consider rattling and grunting more aggressively than you normally would if it seems that the rut is momentarily on hold. Get to your hunting area early, then hunt through the middle of the day and until the last moments of dusk, if legal. And late in the day is a prime time to hunt those food sources I mentioned earlier.

FIND STAGING AREAS

During the middle of the day, scout the edges of fields to find major trails coming into them. Then carefully work your way back into the brush and find a staging area, normally where two or more trails converge. Look for a large track pacing back and forth in this area or possibly a rub or scrape to indicate the presence of a buck. But even if you do not see anything you can definitely identify as buck sign, consider setting up a treestand, ladder stand or tripod where you can watch this area. Make certain that you take advantage of the prevailing breezes and the afternoon and evening sun.

Quite often, bucks will come to these staging areas to check every doe that heads toward the fields along those trails during the late afternoon. And here they can do so without exposing themselves to potential danger from hunters or other bucks. I have taken several good bucks a short distance from a food plot in these staging areas when it seemed that the rut was never going to kick into high gear.

You can do the same thing. The next time when you head to deer camp and all the locals say the rut isn't happening yet, don't despair. Just return to the basics and hunt that much harder and longer. That way you stand good odds for success, even without the rut.

common sense. But you can enhance your setup, I believe, by utilizing a decoy. And when the chips are down on the rut, you need every advantage you can get.

You use either a buck or doe decoy. If I use a doe decoy, I'll set it up a little way down the trail, between the scrape and where I am set up, and douse it with doe-in-heat scent. If I use a buck decoy, I'll set it up fairly close to the scrape and douse the area with buck scent. In either instance, I'll do some soft grunting, either with my mouth or with a call. Remember, never use a decoy during firearms season unless you're absolutely positive that you are the only hunter with permission to deer hunt that piece of property.

Quite often when the rut is going on, but not obvious during the daylight hours, I will spend a considerable amount of time rattling while using a decoy. That way any deer responding will see "a deer" when it comes in, and it will not focus on me. A buck that comes to horns is relying a great deal on its vision. It's looking for other deer. The decoy gives the approaching deer confidence that it's walking or running into a natural situation.

And bucks probably respond best when the rut is close but does aren't quite ready. A lot of hunters refer to this time as

Don't give up on rut hunting tactics late in the season.

Looking for a Fight

PHOTOS BY LARRY HOLJENCIN

Buck fights are sometimes to the death, like the one you're about to witness.

WARNING: The following information is not for the weak-of-heart or hunters who are subject to the forces of buck fever. The North American Hunting Club accepts no responsibility for the adrenaline rush you are about to experience.

Mention the word decoy among a crowd of hunters and you'll see their ears perk up like those on a spooked pack horse. Deer decoys have especially sparked the interest of whitetail hunters searching for a new trick to fool a trophy buck.

Exclusively for members of the North American Hunting Club, we offer this series of action photos that capture the excitement when a deer decoy works. When the posturing threats of a real bone-and-muscle white-tailed buck fail to scare off the intruder, it can get downright violent. Long, spear-like antler tines can inflict serious damage.

Photographer Larry Holjencin set out to the northern Pennsylvania woods in October to capture the interaction between real white-tailed bucks and his Delta Supreme deer decoy. After erecting the decoy, he concealed himself in a deadfall about 35 yards away. His partner, John, then began blowing on a grunt call. Within minutes, the buck emerged from the brush to defend his turf.

As the real deer approached the imposter, it lowered its head and ears in a dominant threatening position. With an explosive hiss, the buck charged. Its powerful neck separated the decoy from its legs and sent it sailing through the air. As soon as the defenseless decoy landed on the ground, the hormone-intoxicated buck administered a thorough thrashing.

When the decoy appeared good and dead, the buck moved on — maybe looking for other sorry souls attempting to swipe does from his turf.

Sure Signs

LARRY WEISHUHN

Though bucks seem to spend considerable time tearing up scrapes and licking branches during the pre-rut, this behavior occurs less frequently when bucks are chasing does during the peak of the rut.

Ask any whitetail hunter what are the most important deer signs to look for when scouting or hunting and the most common answers are rubs and scrapes. On this there seems to be universal agreement.

I'm no different. Whether scouting during post-season, preseason or when hunting a new area, I look for rubs and scrapes. It's difficult to distinguish whether tracks, droppings or beds were made by a buck or doe. With scrapes and rubs, there can be no mistake.

I've spent considerable time in the field during my 50-plus years of hunting and more than 35 years as a wildlife biologist specializing in white-tailed deer. Here's some of what I've learned about rubs and scrapes.

■■■

"I try to do most of my scouting immediately after the deer hunting season closes, while pre-rut and rutting signs are still relatively fresh."

■■■

SCOUT THEM OUT

When and where possible, I try to do most of my scouting immediately after the deer hunting season closes, while pre-rut and rutting signs are still relatively fresh. I also do a fair amount of scouting during the spring turkey seasons that occur only a short time after most bucks have cast their antlers. Then, when possible, I again scout the areas in late summer just as bucks are starting to lose the velvet from their new racks. During this time, deer pay very little attention to humans in the countryside.

Quite often I hunt new areas each fall throughout the continent. Usually I have to rely on the scouting reports of others, and have only a very limited amount of time to scout and hunt. I suspect that many of you do the same.

RUBS

Despite what some people might tell you, you can learn a lot from rubs. Contrary to what many believe, a rub is not always used by the same buck. Several bucks might use the same rub.

Maybe you've heard terms like primary rub, secondary rub, breeding rub and even community rub. To me, either a rub is

Mature bucks often make a rub that they will never return to. Rub lines, however, allow savvy hunters to intercept a buck along its preferred travel route.

active or inactive. Most of the inactive rubs found during the late fall are those a buck happened to use when its velvet was peeling. The rubbing simply hastens the process. Early in fall, bucks might also battle with shrubs and even tall weeds while playing out mock combat scenes. These rubs are seldom, if ever, returned to as the late summer leads to pre-rut activities. Therefore, rubs made during velvet peeling or early in fall are usually inactive rubs.

Active rubs, however, are often found along travel corridors. These could be old logging trails, cattle trails, pasture roads or along edge areas where woods meet fields. Fencelines separating fields are also good places to check for active rubs. In hilly country, you will frequently find rub lines along the bottom of valleys and just below crests of the ridges. When a buck travels through new territory, he might stop and rub on every rub he finds.

It is also quite common for bucks to return to rub on the same sapling or tree year after year. Such perennial rubs generally show scarring from the previous year's use. On several occasions, I have seen the same buck rub on the same tree during a three-year period. Series of rubs, forming a rub line, generally run in somewhat of a line or even a circle.

Do big bucks rub on big trees? I'd like to think so, because my personal observations seem to confirm this. Other serious trophy hunters tend to agree. I like to hunt in areas where rubs are made on trees that are at least eight inches in circumference.

By looking at the surface of the rub, you can also get an idea about the texture and shape of the buck's antlers. A buck with a gnarly rack or one with quite a few sticker points around the bases will make a rub that has several deep grooves in the surface of the rub. If there are only a few, chances are he is making those with his browtines. If the surface of the rub is smooth, chances are the surface of the buck's antlers is quite smooth as well. If there are broken and scarred limbs or underbrush behind where the rub is being made you can get some idea how wide the buck's rack is or how long his tines are. You can also determine which way the buck normally travels while on his rub line. He rubs the same side of the tree that he comes from.

I like to hunt rub lines, but do so mostly during the pre-rut period. After the rut is in full swing, buck movement is helter-skelter, and bucks do not visit rubs as frequently. After the heat of the rut subsides, I again hunt rub lines. During the preseason, when bucks are spending considerable time rubbing, I often use my rattling antlers to imitate a buck working on a rub. I have "rubbed up" some extremely impressive bucks using this technique.

"I like to hunt rub lines, but do so mostly during the pre-rut and post-rut period. After the rut is in full swing, buck movement is helter-skelter, and bucks do not visit rubs as frequently."

When bucks rub, they are not only rubbing their antlers on the tree or sapling, they are also rubbing their forehead glands on the surface of the rub and marking it with their distinct scent. If you watch a buck make a rub, you will notice that he rubs for a while and then smells the surface of the rub. In the same respect, when a buck approaches an active rub, he generally first smells the rub before touching his antlers to the tree.

Based on my observations, it seems that old bucks spend considerably less time rubbing than do the middle-aged bucks that also do most of the breeding. Even though bucks truly are individuals, I am convinced that many bucks more than four or five years old are more concerned about survival than they are about rutting activities.

Rub areas signify that a buck is comfortable traveling here. He might do so again soon.

Scrapes probably let down more hunters than any other form of sign. Don't bet the farm on him coming back.

SCRAPES

Making and freshening scrapes are, for the most part, buck activities. However, on rare occasions I have seen does visit scrapes and do everything you would expect from a buck, including chewing or nuzzling the overhanging branch, actively scraping the ground and dribbling urine in the scrape. Such occurrences are rare. Contrary to popular belief, I seriously doubt that they were there to leave their "calling card" as they approached estrus.

I do not believe that a scrape belongs to any one buck. Nor am I a big believer in categorizing scrapes as primary, secondary and breeding scrapes. Like rubs, I believe a scrape is either active or inactive. I am convinced that some bucks make scrapes each fall without ever intending to return to them. I have also seen bucks make scrapes without the presence of an overhanging limb.

On the other hand, I have watched bucks return to the same scrape year after year. I have been watching one particular scrape now for nine years. Each year it has been extremely active. The pawed-out area below the overhanging limb is several inches deep. During those nine years, it has varied in diameter from 18 inches to eight feet. The year the scrape was the deepest and the widest occurred when the deer population had an abundance of three- and four-year-old bucks.

Research tells us that most of the scraping activity takes place during the cover of night. In the case of the long-lived scrape that I just mentioned, I have seen as many as 13 different bucks actively work that scrape during the course of a single day during the pre-rut period. How many bucks actually used the scrape? I wish I knew. Interestingly, four of those 13 bucks were trophy-sized animals — easily what many hunters would classify as "dominant" bucks. In fact, in some parts of the country, all of the bucks that used the scrape during that one period of daylight might have been considered dominant bucks. The smallest buck to use the scrape while I was there appeared to be a two-year-old eight-point with about a 15-inch spread. The biggest buck was a non-typical with 18 easily-counted points. I'd guess he was a five- or six-year-old deer.

■ ■ ■

"I am convinced that many bucks more than four or five years old are more concerned about survival than they are about rutting activities."

■ ■ ■

Like rubs, scrapes are often found along travel corridors leading to and from feeding and bedding areas and along the edges of prime feeding spots. I have seen considerably more scraping activity during the pre-rut than any other time. When the bucks are chasing does during the peak of the rut, they might or might not take time to visit scrapes. I strongly suspect that they will freshen scrapes, but only if they happen by them while they are looking for receptive does. When the rut is in full swing, I seldom see bucks working scrapes, nor have I seen many does very near scrapes during this time. As the rut period starts to wane, bucks seem to return to actively work scrapes for a while.

I always try to rattle antlers near where I find a large scrape or a series of scrapes. Bucks generally respond to horns in these areas. I don't think it is because they are protecting "their" scrapes, but rather that scrapes in an area means good odds of multiple adult bucks somewhere in the vicinity.

We continue to learn about the nature and science of rubs and scrapes.

We will likely never really know precisely why white-tailed bucks make rubs and scrapes. You can, however, be certain of one thing. If you find rubs and scrapes, you have found bucks.

Big buck rub, big buck . . . sometimes.

CHAPTER 5

Hunting Big Bucks

This talk of trophies, of truly big bucks, is touchy stuff. So let's be clear on the use of the word "trophy." As it relates to this chapter, we'll equate trophies with record books — bucks with antlers that measure large enough to qualify for a particular category of some record book. That is generally what "trophy" hunters seek: mature white-tailed bucks with big antlers.

Anything wrong with that? Only if you believe that a musky angler holding out for a 40-pounder for the wall is also wrong. Trophy hunters raise the bar. It is a personal choice, usually not one they try to push on others. It requires extreme discipline and hard hunting. It means hundreds of deer, some of them fine bucks, will walk on as the hunter waits for a particular animal. And, as most trophy hunters quickly point out, those passed-up animals are deer that other hunters will have a chance to shoot someday. Much like the 20-pound muskies the musky hunter searching for a trophy releases.

Many deer hunters say any deer is a trophy. And that's really to say that all wild animals are deserving of our respect and reverence. Ask any deer hunter, even the most devout trophy hunter, whether he considers his first deer a trophy. He'll undoubtedly count it as one — maybe his finest ever. Some, however, take the trophy hunting mentality too far and begin to look at does and younger bucks as "lesser" animals. And as they trip over themselves with tape measure in hand, they forget about venison roasts, brilliant autumn colors, the joy of hunting with friends and family, hunting hard and all the little things leading up to a big buck.

Here's to perspective and to dreams of giant whitetails . . .

■ ■ ■

Owner's Manual to the Next World Record

JIM SHOCKEY

Somewhere, sometime in the not-too-distant future, someone is going to tag the new world record typical white-tailed buck. That buck and the hunter who takes him will gain instant, international notoriety.

Because you are a deer hunter, you could be the one. Far-fetched as that might be, think about it for a second anyway. What if you beat the odds, would you know what to do?

Imagine you're on stand late one fall afternoon. Suddenly, you catch a glimpse of the most magnificent buck you've ever seen. It happens more quickly than it takes to tell it; thankfully so, because you don't have time to develop buck fever before you aim and the huge animal drops. As you approach, the antlers seem to grow.

By the time you reach down and touch the buck, you're aware that it is very special indeed. You are excited, but still manage to remember to tag him immediately. Realizing he is too large for you to drag alone, you head out of the bush and flag down some help. Just as you reach your truck, a vehicle drives down the road. Two hunters stop to chat, and you ask them for help.

A good bit later, as the sun sets, you close the tailgate of your truck. The buck is safe and sound. So for the next hour you relive the hunt with your new friends, explaining in detail how you took the buck with one shot. Happy to vicariously hunt the buck with you, the two hunters congratulate you over and over. Eventually, you part company. You wish them good luck as they drive away, but as their tail lights disappear, you remember that you never did ask their names.

During the hour drive home, you try your best to recall what it was you read about measuring antlers. By the time you pull into your garage, it's getting late, but you feel you have to call someone. You call a friend who says he'll be right over, but since it's poker night, he asks to bring the guys along, too. Of course, the more the merrier.

By the time the guys show up, it's near midnight, but you can't sleep anyway. During the course of the celebration, one of the guys says he knows how to measure your buck for the record book.

With bated breath you await the verdict. When the score comes, you are disappointed. The fellow, puffed out with importance, points his beer at the buck and explains to you that while it is a big buck, it doesn't quite make "the book." "Oh well," you reason, "it's still big enough to have mounted."

But then the guys talk you out of it. It costs a fortune, they tell you. Better to just save the antlers and have them mounted on a plaque. So the next morning you cut the antlers off and take the carcass to the meat processor. Until the butcher calls a week later, you pretty much forget the whole thing.

When you go to pick up the meat and ask for the hide, the kid at the counter points to a pile in the corner and says to take whichever one you want or leave it for a donation to the local habitat project. On the same trip, you drop the antlers by the taxidermist.

Still with me? Granted, you might do things differently. Maybe you'd measure the buck yourself or decide to mount the deer in spite of your buddies' advice, but for the most part, the sequence is pretty typical. So what happens after you take the buck to the taxidermist?

First, he informs you that you might have killed a new world record buck, and then he calls some other hunters to come over with their cameras and confirm it. They do, and within 24 hours the story is out in a local newspaper. You were never interviewed for the article. Within a day, your phone begins to ring — writers and antler buyers. They want the story and the antlers. "Will you give an exclusive? Will you sign a contract? Will you sell the antlers?"

The story appears nationally the next day. Funny thing is, you still haven't given an interview. The telephone calls increase in frequency and insistence. "How about a television show? Will you endorse this? How about that? Can we use the buck for a sport show? Have you had it scored officially yet?"

■ ■ ■

"Imagine you're on stand late one fall afternoon. Suddenly, you catch a glimpse of the most magnificent buck you've ever seen."

■ ■ ■

You're overwhelmed. You sign a contract or two, taking what seems like a fair offer — a free taxidermy mount in exchange for an interview. Then you start to receive the strange calls. The first one accuses you of being a poaching publicity hound. A day later a story appears in the local paper saying you are being investigated for poaching. It's the first you've heard of it. The next day the poaching story runs nationally. A lawyer calls. You are being sued for misrepresenting yourself in endorsing a product. You explain that you never endorsed a product as far as you know. He says you better get a lawyer.

When you hang up, your doorbell rings. It's the game warden with several policemen and reporters. The questions fly. "Did you kill your buck at night? We have affidavits from some poker players that say you arrived home with your buck around midnight."

"Not true! I mean true!" You try to explain that yes, you came home late, but you killed the buck during the day.

He's big. You might not know just how big. Better safe than sorry.

"Do you have witnesses?"

"Yes! No!" You explain about the two nameless guys who helped you drag out your buck.

"Do you have pictures to corroborate your story? Did you have permission to hunt on the land?"

"It was public land," you protest.

"Can you prove it? Was your buck killed out of season? May we see the cape to confirm the buck was in its fall coat?"

You try to explain about the pile of hides. They confiscate the antlers until the matter is resolved. That night you sit in front of your television watching the sharks feeding on your formerly snow-white reputation. Your father phones to disown you. Your girlfriend calls to say it's over. Your dog won't let you touch him. You look at yourself in the mirror and wonder what you did wrong.

ED KOBERSTEIN'S EXPERIENCE

Now this scenario might seem far-fetched, but it isn't as exaggerated as you might believe. Ed Koberstein, well known to NAHC members as the man who harvested what was thought to be a potential new world record whitetail in 1991, will tell you that shooting such a buck is far more trouble than it's worth.

In Koberstein's case, the question of poaching came up as an ugly rumor and was dutifully checked out and dismissed by local conservation officers. What's more, one of the very first written stories about the buck was printed without Koberstein's consent. Another twist to the story had to do with one of the hunters with Koberstein that day. It seems that he took photos of Koberstein and his buck but wouldn't let Koberstein have any of the photos to use in the many magazine articles being written about the buck. Maybe that hunter thought he could sell them for piles of money if the buck did, indeed, turn out to be a world record.

Even after countering all the allegations, Koberstein ended up with more problems. His buck was officially scored by experienced Boone and Crockett Club scorer Randy Bean. However, shortly after the buck was officially scored, Koberstein received a letter from B&C saying that the buck would have to be re-scored by a panel of scorers chaired by another official scorer of their choosing. Today, the buck holds its place in the record book, but it is far from a world record.

A HUGE BUCK: WHAT TO DO

Let's return to your stand that beautiful fall evening when that magnificent buck appeared. Shoot him like you did and then tag him, but this time when you walk up to him and realize he is special, forget celebrating, forget excitement, forget every natural human reaction. Think of one thing: documentation! Somehow, you absolutely have to document the event. Not only the fact that it happened, but that it happened at that exact time and that exact place. For this you must have a camera; better yet — a still camera *and* a video camera. You need a camera; if you don't have one, get one. Buy it from the farmer down the road if need be, but get a camera!

Take the camera and start snapping photos of the buck. Always have at least two rolls of film for insurance. Take a bunch of shots of the buck, including several close-ups of its face to show its eyes are not sunken. If possible, try to include something in the photos that will prove the date. Anything will help, but if you had the day's newspaper in the truck, get it and include it in the close-ups. As you leave the scene to get help, take a couple of photos from some distance away to show the location. Be sure the animal can be seen in the photo.

Go back to your truck and this time, when the vehicle with the two hunters drives up, ask them if they will take a photo of you with the buck you killed. Remember, those two hunters are your best defense against accusations of hunting illegally. They will know your buck was freshly killed, where it was killed, when it was killed, and that circumstances dictate that you

were the one who killed the buck. As sad a commentary as it is, at some point you'll need to address every one of these questions. Get them to take pictures of you with the buck . . . lots of pictures. There is no such thing as too many. Get them to take photos from every angle. Keep the background uncluttered. Get one of the hunters to take a couple of pictures of you and the other hunter with the buck.

The situation gets sticky if one of your helpers pulls out his own camera. The last thing you need are unauthorized stories. Suggest to the fellow that you need even more pictures and offer to buy his film. If he won't sell it to you, make sure you are in every picture he takes of the buck. Legally, he cannot publish photos of you if you have not given him permission.

■■■

"Remember, it's a small fraternity and one that frowns upon the exploitation of a game animal for personal gain."

■■■

After the photo session, it's time to take the buck back to your vehicle. Once you are back at your truck, get the hunters to give you their names, addresses and phone numbers. Also, get them to sign a statement of fact. Any paper, even the back of your cartridge box, will do. Write down the particulars of the hunt: i.e., time, location, date and how many points you believe are on the rack. Mention that the buck was freshly killed. When the hunters leave, they might think you are paranoid, but you'll have answers for the conservation officers when they come knocking.

By now it will be dark, but you still have to show the buck to a few more people. Drive it to the nearest farm and show the farmer. Get his name and number and get him to sign your piece of paper saying you showed up at his house at whatever time it happens to be. Remember, don't allow anyone else to take pictures. Now take the buck directly to the nearest police station or, even better, to a conservation officer. Even if you have to go right to the man's house, do it. He might complain, but that'll stop when he lays eyes on your buck. Make sure that whoever you show the buck to looks closely and notes that it has been dead for several hours. The idea is to discredit any accusations of poaching. Have the officer check your license and tag to confirm that all is in order and then, like before, get him to sign a paper saying he did so.

PHOTOS ARE KEY

Until morning comes, you have done all you can. Don't do any more that night. Don't call all your friends and invite them over for a party. First thing in the morning, call a photographer. You need a professional and should be prepared to pay. Unfortunately, this is also the weak link in the chain. The person who snaps the picture actually owns the copyright to the photo. In your case, it is imperative that the photographer knows that you are to get the rolls of film (slide film) as they come out of the camera. Tell him that the only way you'll hire him is if he'll sign a paper stating that he relinquishes copyright of the photos to you.

For these photos, the background has to be uncluttered and wilderness-looking. Drive the buck to where the background is suitably wild. Skyline the antlers or have them displayed against snow. Remember, brushy backgrounds are out. Take at least ten 36-exposure rolls. Have the photographer bracket the exposures (he'll know what that means). These are the shots that will appear in the magazines later and perhaps in advertisements for products that you might be asked to endorse. They have to be good.

Only after you have posed for so many pictures that your face hurts from smiling can you finally call it quits. Take your buck home and skin it out, taking care to keep the hide intact and attached to the head and antlers. Make room in your freezer for the cape and antlers, and throw them in.

SCORING . . . AND PHILOSOPHY

Now you can put your feet up. It's okay to take a break, because it's time to go underground. If you want to tell your close friends and family, then do so, but with no interviews and no pictures. At this point, you need the advice from the powers that be. Place a call to Boone and Crockett Club headquarters and ask what they suggest (B&C, Dept. NAH, Old Milwaukee Depot, 250 Station Dr., Missoula, MT 59801, 406-542-1888). They'll be able to recommend an official scorer in good standing and will arrange for you to receive a "how-to" guide about scoring. If, after receiving your B&C scoring directions and green scoring your buck, you find that the antlers are going to score above the B&C minimums, you should make arrangements for an official scoring of the rack. The buck cannot be officially scored until 60 days after it was taken. You'll need the time anyway to decide what it is you want to have happen in your life for the next year.

Do you want to quit your job and do guest appearances at every outdoor show from coast to coast? Do you want your smiling face plastered beside this and that hunting product? Do you want to capitalize on your good fortune? There are those who believe that the hunter who shoots the next world record typical buck will have the opportunity to parlay his good luck into $1 million.

Still, the "who's who" in the hunting world will be real touchy if you come across as a gold digger. Remember, it's a small fraternity and one that frowns upon the exploitation of a game animal for personal gain. Hunting is not about money and never will be. Perhaps instead, you should think about the millions of young hunters you'll be able to reach because of your accomplishment. We could use a hero in the hunting world. Why not you?

Regardless of what side of the fence you decide to stand on, there are three more things you should know. First, if your buck doesn't soundly beat the old world record, expect B&C officials to announce a re-score of the existing world record; unless your buck is several inches larger than the Hanson buck, it's my prediction that you'll only be king for a day. Second, call NAHC headquarters. Third, ask them to put you in touch with me.

Great in-the-field shots are always valuable.

Five Seconds to Success

LARRY WEISHUHN

Quick! He'll be gone in a second! How big? Big enough!

A mature, hunter-wise white-tailed buck seldom gives a hunter more than five seconds to spot him, evaluate his antlers, estimate the distance and make a killing shot. That doesn't seem like very much time, does it? It isn't! If you are interested in taking mature bucks, you better learn to work fast. How you use those precious seconds can spell the difference between success and failure.

The first step in taking a good whitetail is hunting areas where mature bucks exist. However, hunting the right areas still doesn't guarantee that you'll see big bucks. You need to know where and how to look for deer. Too often we look for calendar poses and expect to see deer standing in the open. It hardly ever works out this way. It is a far better approach to expect to see only parts of deer, like the twitch of an ear or a tail, sunlight glinting off of an antler or the dark spots of a deer's nose or eyes.

EVALUATING A RACK

As soon as you see a deer, concentrate on its head to quickly identify whether it is a buck or doe. If antlers are present, try to determine the number of points, tine length, main beam length, mass and spread. Some hunters are interested in number of points, some in spread, others in the overall size of the rack, and still others in the Boone and Crockett Club score. I want a mature deer with antlers that please me.

While looking at the buck's head, determine if both sides of the rack are present, then check if both sides are fairly equal in size. The next step is to count the number of points off the main beam. Look at one side of the rack. If the main beam has a brow tine and one primary tine, the buck is likely a six-point. If there is a brow tine and two primary points coming off the main beam, the buck is likely an eight-point. For each additional primary point, the total increases by two: three primaries, 10-point; four primaries, 12-point and so on.

After you have quickly estimated the number of typical points, look for any "kicker" or non-

You shouldn't be hesitating here, either. Even though you're only getting a head-on view, there's enough to tell you that you ought to squeeze the trigger when the first good opportunity presents itself.

typical points. To me, kicker points add to the beauty of a rack, but beauty is in the eye of the beholder. If you are interested in B&C scores, you can quickly estimate a rack's gross score by knowing a few simple, fairly standard measurements on a deer's head. Compare these measurements to estimate tine length, main beam length (which comprise the greater part of the B&C scores), circumference and inside spread. These comparison measurements include: the length of a deer's ear (normally eight inches from tip to where it attaches to the neck and six inches from the opening of the ear to the tip); eye to nose (from the forward edge of the eye to the tip of the nose), which averages about seven to eight inches; ear tip to ear tip spread when the ears are in an erect position, about 16 to 17 inches (although it varies from region to region); and the circumference of the deer's eye, which is about four inches. With these "knowns" you can quickly estimate the B&C gross score.

If you are interested in a mature buck, quickly look past the antlers at the deer's face, neck and body. Young bucks have relatively tight skin about their face, and their muscles are not yet fully developed. In addition, young bucks have skinny necks during the fall breeding season. Mature bucks, those 4 years and older, have more fully developed bodies. In the fall, their necks are swollen. They have a fair amount of loose skin about their face, including loose skin hanging under their jaw line. The mature buck might be slightly pot-bellied, and his legs might appear too short for his body. Also, most mature bucks have darkly stained hocks during the breeding season.

Let's say we have spotted a buck. His neck is swollen past the width of his jaw. He has loose skin about his face, and his hocks are darkly stained. A quick check tells you the buck has both antlers present, with three primary tines, and a brow tine on each side. To begin the B&C gross score guess, estimate the total inches of antler present on one side. It appears the brow tine is half as long as the buck's ear, or about four inches. The back tine is as long as the overall length of the buck's ear, or about eight inches. The next tine forward is approximately the same length. The front tine is about the same length as the brow tine, or four inches. The main beam is about three times the length of the eye to nose measurement, or about 21 inches. Each of the four circumference measurements are equal to the circumference of the deer's eye, about four inches. The base circumference is a little larger, and the front measurement between the third and fourth point is a little smaller, but it appears the measurement averages about four inches for a total of 16 inches (B&C measurements include four circumference measurements on both sides).

Quickly add the numbers 4+8+8+4+21+16 for a total of 61 inches. Double that figure, because the other side is approximately equal, for a total of 122. The buck turns to look at you. The inside spread of the main beams is just beyond the erect forward ears, or about 17 inches. Add the accumulated measurements of both sides of the rack to the inside spread and the gross estimated score is 139 B&C points.

MAKING THE SHOT COUNT

Practice on mounted deer heads during the off-season. You'll quickly learn what a rack will score. If the buck interests you, you must next estimate the range. If you are hunting with a bow, your range is extremely limited. If you shoot a blackpowder rifle, shotgun or revolver, you are limited to about 100-yard shots. If you shoot a rifle or one of the single-shot handguns chambered for the rifle cartridges, the opportunity for longer shots exists. With my rifles and handguns, I prefer to use variable scopes in the 3.5-10X range with good light-gathering abilities and duplex-style crosshairs. With my scopes, if the power setting is on 5X, at 100 yards a large deer standing broadside is bracketed between the broad portion of the crosshairs from the front of the chest to the back of the rump. If the deer is bracketed in this manner or bigger, I immediately know the deer is 100 yards or less away. If the deer is 300 yards away it will be bracketed between the broad portion of the crosshairs with the power setting on 8X. Practice at the rifle range using life-sized deer targets to see where your variable scope "brackets" a deer.

A better option still is to purchase a laser rangefinder available from companies like Bushnell, Swarovski and Nikon. These excellent optics provide one-yard accuracy out to distances of 400, 600, 800 yards and farther. That doesn't increase my effective range, but it does eliminate those range-estimating errors of 50 to 75 yards that can mean the difference between a perfect hit and a miss out there beyond 250 yards or so. And since these units can give you a reading in a second or so, you'll save precious time that you'd waste by trying to bracket a deer in your riflescope. By knowing where your rifle is sighted-in and where a particular load will strike a target at varying distances, you greatly increase your odds of taking a big buck.

Ten-point frame, heavy, tall, long beams . . . Time's up. Shoot!

I also shoot from a solid rest if at all possible! Even though I have the chance to see hundreds of big bucks each year, they still make me excited, and I want all the help I can get to make a killing shot. Lots of things to think about and do in just five seconds? Perhaps, but when you're talking big bucks, the clock is definitely ticking!

Big Bucks at All Costs

LARRY WEISHUHN

Images of a buck like this are merely hazy dreams for most deer hunters.

Here's a flash for you: big whitetails excite me! NAHC members realize that's no secret. Like a fair number of you, I got into hunting whitetails when whitetails weren't necessarily "cool." Even during my younger years in the 1950s, I knew that someday I would be a white-tailed deer biologist. Naturally, my avocation was then, and always would be, hunting whitetails!

It was about 25 years later that I had an opportunity to work on a video production with a Texan, John Wootters. I had first met Wootters while I was a biologist with the Texas Parks & Wildlife Department. My assignment at that time was to work with landowners and sportsmen in establishing and helping to maintain quality white-tailed deer programs on their private property. Wootters had been a hero of mine ever since the middle 1960s when I read his magazine article titled, "The Art of Brush Hunting."

Wootters, in many respects, deserves credit for the current interest in "quality" deer hunting, or, more specifically, hunting for "quality" bucks. My old friend did for white-tailed deer hunting what Jack O'Connor had done for sheep hunting during the golden age of big game hunting. Wootters' book *Hunting Trophy Bucks* was the first of its kind and it remains a classic. The video that Wootters and I worked on together, *Whitetails, Judging Trophies*, was done in conjunction with Jerry Smith. Smith, another fellow Texan, also deserves a great amount of the credit for today's interest in quality deer because of his excellent cover photos of monster bucks that appeared on publications throughout the 1970s and '80s. It was quite a team! When I was asked to work with both men on a video about field-judging antlers and aging white-tailed deer, I could not say "yes" quickly nor loudly enough! I am proud to say that our video is still considered one of the most authoritative, educational and entertaining on the subject.

CHANGING TIMES

Since the first rumblings of interest in big whitetails, several things have changed. Back then, finding huge white-tailed deer was not easy. Few bucks lived long enough to reach huge proportions. Sure, just like today, a lot of young bucks were taken by hunters. But poor habitat had more to do with the lack of large bucks. Things are different now.

More hunters and managers have gotten into quality white-tailed deer management, habitat has greatly improved, and bucks in many areas are now being given a chance to mature in the presence of year-round nutrition. The size of bucks is

This is a much more common sight in the deer woods. Not every deer you see is going to be a big buck. Enjoy all deer!

definitely increasing, and the Boone and Crockett Club offers proof. According to a recent review of B&C records, nearly 74 percent of the record book's total entries were taken in the past 20 years. Even more amazing is the fact that nearly 55 percent of B&C entries were recorded in the past decade.

Quantity has increased along with the quality of whitetails in North America. The animal's range is expanding. Quite frankly, the interest in whitetails and whitetail hunting has never been more keen. Witness the increase in the number of hunting publications devoted entirely to whitetails. These days, too, practically every state that has white-tailed deer has its own record book. With the improvement of whitetail habitat, nearly all the other game and non-game species have benefited as well.

But there might also be a dark side to all this, especially when we focus on deer antlers. During the past several years, we have seen several big buck scams: racks from Canada were claimed to have been taken in Texas and Mexico. Giant sheds were allegedly mounted on a dead deer later claimed to have been taken in a southeastern state. We have also seen errors in judgment made by well-known hunters who did not think that they would be considered good deer hunters unless they took huge bucks every year, no matter the cost, ethics or laws. An even more disturbing trend is the captive breeding of whitetails for

■■■

"More hunters and managers have gotten into quality white-tailed deer management, habitat has greatly improved, and bucks in many areas are now being given a chance to mature."

■■■

trophy production. Across the country, domestic animal husbandry has infiltrated the whitetail world. Bucks bred in captivity are selling for $300,000 or more, but the big money is in semen straws, male offspring and prime lineage does. In Texas alone, individual deer auctions typically generate up to $1 million per month. The *San Antonio News* reported that the state's deer breeding industry pumps more than $2.8 billion into the state's economy annually.

SOME SURPRISING THOUGHTS

I have been involved in such projects, but no longer am. I'd much rather see the money currently spent on trying to

Some areas just flat out won't grow Boone and Crockett bucks. Should that diminish the deer hunting experience in these places?

alter the genetics of a deer herd instead spent on habitat improvement and bringing new hunters into our great sport of deer hunting.

In some instances we are seeing deer hunters with different goals and standards: hunters more interested in the size of a buck's antlers than the quality of the hunting experience. This type of individual concerns and saddens me. Thankfully, they are by far in the minority, but they do exist.

A few years ago, I was on a hunt with an individual who wanted a record-book whitetail in the worst way. After exhaustive research, he found a ranch that had such a buck, one that the ranch owner thought might give the hunter a chance if the hunter hunted for at least a week. As luck would have it, that is what happened. The buck was a magnificent typical 12-point — wide, tall, massive; a buck of which dreams are made. After five days of hard hunting, the individual took the buck. The successful "hunter" was ecstatic!

While the ranch manager was taking pictures, the hunter was busily scoring the buck. When the score was tallied and deducts subtracted, the rack fell two-eighths of an inch shy of the magic 170 points for entry into the all-time B&C records. At that point, the hunter got up and started cursing and saying that he did not want the deer. "He's not record-book," the hunter said. "I don't want to see any more of him."

That person did not deserve to be called a hunter. I was sick and hoped that I'd never again share a hunting camp with him or anyone like him. I hoped that he'd quit hunting.

Maybe that is one of several reasons that I was so tickled when Milo Hanson, a farmer from Biggar, Saskatchewan took the current world-record typical whitetail. Milo was not a trophy hunter — just your average deer hunter. I've had the opportunity to eat dinner and visit with both Milo and his wife. In my opinion, he deserves to have taken the world record, and it could not have been taken by a more gracious, genuine person — someone who truly loves hunting.

Sure, I love big-antlered bucks, but I generally hunt for mature and over-the-hill bucks, deer that have survived several hunting seasons. Sometimes really old bucks don't have the best-scoring antlers. I don't care. Do I always take a buck? I wish I could say "yes," but that is not the case. I get to hunt numerous places each year where the potential of taking a really large-antlered buck exists. I plan it that way! But it doesn't always happen.

Do I have to shoot a big buck to have a successful hunt? No way! The quality of a hunt should have nothing to do with the score of a deer's rack. If it does, then perhaps you ought to re-evaluate why you hunt in the first place.

CHAPTER 6

Living the Hunt

At its best, whitetail hunting stirs in us feelings and emotions buried under heaps of computers-working-commuting-stress-mortgage payments-asphalt & concrete . . . to everything else that makes life what it is today. In deer country, we become what we are at our most basic: hunters. It might take several days in a fine deer camp to find it. But it's there in all of us, and it's reassuring to know that we can still step back in the midst of a life that usually races ahead at breakneck speed.

This chapter is about simplicity. It is about realizing that it's OK to say that deer hunting is fun. Because it most certainly is. Deer camp is a place to laugh loudly, and old deer stands are fine places to think about those things that are really important to all of us. Society has a way of sweeping us away in streams of information and deadlines and work of all kinds. Deer hunting has a way of bringing us back.

We've endeavored in this chapter to take you hunting, both for fun and serious reflection. We'll have succeeded if, by the time you turn the final page of this book, you have laughed a little and thought a lot about what deer hunting means to you and your family.

Here's to many great seasons. Remember to keep the whitetail hunting tradition alive. Let's pass it on and leave the whitetail woods even better than we found them . . .

■ ■ ■

A Question of Ethics

JOHN SLOAN

Shadows stretching across the yard, the old man sat peacefully in the shade of the chinaberry tree. At the man's right hand, sitting squarely on an old handcrafted oak stool, a quart jar of iced tea with plenty of lemon and sugar sweated in the sun. At his feet, a young puppy dreamed of days to come, kicking its back legs from time to time, probably chasing birds in golden fields of a far-off land.

The man sighed contentedly as he rubbed the Cornhusker's lotion into his hands. That last bluegill spined a fin under one fingernail. Those things can hurt like the dickens, he thought. His grandson, now 12 and full of himself, finished putting the last of the rods and reels in the garage and came to sit beside him, a can of pop in his left hand, worm dirt on both.

What an afternoon. Fillets from 35 thick bream were draining in the sink. All but a double handful would go in the freezer. The rest would be supper, along with fresh tomatoes from the garden and some good, green onions and fries and maybe cornbread. His mouth watered and he sipped his tea.

The boy slurped his pop. "Gramps," he said, "just what is *ethics?*"

The old man swallowed his tea and looked at the boy. "Ethics? What brought that on?"

"You know I took that hunter education course last week," the boy said. "The instructor talked a lot about ethics, but he didn't exactly explain what ethics is. Does that mean obeying all the laws?"

"Lemme study on this a minute, boy. Lemme see can I explain it better. See, ethics is not easy to explain nor easy to understand. It's kinda like a special sunrise. Hard to put to words.

"Now this afternoon, we caught how many bluegill? Fifty, maybe 75? According to the law, we could have kept 70, right?"

The boy nodded and started to speak.

"But," the old man broke in quickly, "we only kept 35. Why is that, you reckon?"

"Well, you said we only needed 35 to make a couple good messes," the boy replied. "That was all we could use."

"Right," the old man nodded. "We could have kept 70 and been legal. But that would have been hoggish. It wouldn't have been ethical even though it was legal. So, ethics doesn't always mean the same as legal. See what I mean?"

The boy sucked some pop and scratched the pup's ears. "I see that, but does that mean ethical means keeping less than the limit?"

"No son, that ain't exactly it, either," the man said. "In some ways, ethical means keeping only what you can use. But that is just one example. Here's another: You recall last year when we went dove hunting and that dove lit right over your head? You recall, I didn't let you shoot it? See, you could have shot it. It would have been legal. But it wouldn't have been ethical, for that dove would not have had a chance. It wouldn't have been sporting."

The boy looked up. "I understood that," he said. "It wasn't fair to the bird." The pup nudged the boy's hand.

"Right," the man continued. "And remember when you killed that nice doe last fall and wanted to drive all over showing her off. That was plumb legal, and lots of folks would have done it. But it wasn't ethical. You recall what I told you?"

"You said that most didn't give a tinker's damn about my deer, and it wasn't right to rub their noses in the gut pile," the boy said. "That it was fine to be proud of my deer, but that it was a personal thing and the doe should be treated with respect."

"That's exactly right," the man said. "Now think on this. This fall, when you come to hunting camp, some days you'll be hunting alone. Won't be nobody but you there to make decisions of what's right and what's wrong. An old deer comes along, only you decide if you have a shot or not. Ain't no law says you can't shoot one in the butt. Is it the right thing to do? Is it ethical to shoot an old deer in the butt?"

The boy was silent, thinking about the situation and stroking the pup's belly. "I guess not," he finally said. "It wouldn't be fair to the deer. I'd wait for a good, broadside shot."

"Now think on this." The old man sipped his tea while he formed the words. "You found that big deer crossing at the head of the draw last year, and I said it would be your stand. I won't hunt it. It's yours. But what if when you get there opening day, some other hunter is already set up

Silence. The pup sprawled full length in the boy's lap. "Is it first-come, first-served?" the old man quizzed and waited for the boy's thoughts.

"I guess it would be," the boy said. "But what is the ethical thing to do? Should I explain that I thought it was my stand and ask him to move?"

The old man chuckled. "Reverse the situation, boy. What if you were there first? What would you want another hunter to do in that situation?"

"Well, I'd want him to just go quietly away and find another spot," the boy said. "I'd want him to try and not disturb my stand."

The old man stretched and smiled. "Right. That's the ethical thing to do," he said.

The boy grinned. "So ethics is kinda like the Golden Rule, do unto others as you would have them do unto you."

"Yes," the man said. "It's that and more. It's doing what is right and what is responsible and fair. It's more than that, too. And I'll tell you, son, it's too dadgum hard for an old man like me to explain. Ethics, son, is the way you are. The way you live. The way you think. With good examples and good teachers, you'll understand as you grow. And son, you've got good teachers. I've seen to that."

The old man searched for a match, filled his pipe and got it sucking and gurgling to suit him. "You know Mrs. Beckman, Paulie's mother?"

The boy nodded. "She and Paulie were in my hunter education class. I wondered what she was doing there. Paulie's a year older than me. He likes to hunt, but his dad was sick and couldn't take him last year."

"I know," the old man said. "That's why Sue — Mrs. Beckman — was taking the class. See, Paul, that's Paulie's dad, has cancer. They caught it late. It looks as though there isn't much they can do for him. Sue — Mrs. Beckman — she knows Paulie wants to hunt and is figurin' on takin' him next fall. Trouble is, she doesn't know the woods and doesn't really have much of any place to take him." The old man leaned back and looked across the field where a mockingbird was dive-bombing a transient crow.

After a bit, the boy looked up from the pup. "Why couldn't they go with us?" he asked his grandfather. "On the juvenile hunt, it will be just me and you at the camp. There'll be plenty of room. I can show them where to set up. Maybe they could hunt down by the big slough or maybe even I could let Paulie hunt that good trail at the head of the draw."

The old man rubbed something off his forehead and managed to sneak a finger to the corner of his eye. "Why yes, I 'spect they could," he said. "I hadn't thought of that. That would be a nice thing to do, an ethical thing, I reckon. I'll mention it next time I see Sue," he nodded.

there? What do you do? Remember boy, we don't own that land."

The boy piped up, "I'd tell him that was my place and he'd have to move. I found it first."

"How do you know you found it first?" the man asked. "Lemme get this straight. You figger you're the first person to ever see that trail? Son, think on that a minute."

"But it's my stand," the boy pleaded. "You said it was."

"Yes, I did, but was it mine to give? I don't own that land. As far as I'm concerned, it is your stand. But I can't speak for the other hunters who might have found it. And most likely, they found it before you. Maybe they figger it's their stand. How do you deal with that ethically?"

Wonders of the Whitetail

TOM CARPENTER

It's easy to get jaded.

With regards to white-tailed deer, I know the precise moment I realized it had happened. I wasn't hunting on that snowless winter day, but jogging. A mile from my house, I glanced to my left and spotted it — a whitetail, standing perfectly still not 15 yards away in a tiny patch of woods.

Thirty years ago, the sighting would have taken my breath away. At this moment all I thought was, "Oh, deer."

Then I stopped in my tracks and thought again: "Oh, *Deer!*"

I marveled at the doe's complete beauty and utter grace — half-cocked front hoof frozen elegantly in mid-stride, snow-white throat patch stark against her gray coat, ears perked up at full attention, shiny black nose working the breeze.

After drinking in her beauty for a few moments I continued on my way because she was getting a little nervous and I didn't want to spook her onto the road.

Depending on your age you may or may not believe this, but there was a time when spotting a deer was exciting, and to shoot one was a real event. But now, before catching myself in the act, I was hardly even taking notice of this magnificent creature.

It made me a little sad. Whitetails are abundant, but sometimes commonplace. Seeing deer, whether you're hunting or not, isn't always a big deal. And placing excessive value on only the biggest bucks has relegated other whitetails in the herd to secondary status.

Stopping to admire that lovely doe changed the way I look at whitetails, and started bringing me back to my deer hunting roots — when deer weren't a commodity, and just seeing a whitetail was cause for celebration. Whitetails are still the fascinating creatures they always were — worthy of our excitement, attention, fascination and wonder.

WONDERS OF RANGE

What other animal is so highly successful under such varying conditions? The whitetail's adaptability calls for our respect. Whitetails thrive from Venezuela, Peru and Ecuador in South America, through Central America and Mexico, across the United States from east to west and north to south, up to the northern bush of Manitoba, Saskatchewan and Alberta. Whitetails have been spotted as far north as Great Slave Lake.

Now *that's* adaptable — an animal that can thrive in tropical forests, desert scrub, wide-open prairies, wooded foothills, tall mountains, intensively farmed ground, even suburbs and cities . . . from the equator to the tundra.

A whitetail in full gallop can bound up to 30 feet, and reach speeds up to 35 m.p.h.

Once, in the mountains outside of Puerto Vallarta, Mexico, my family and I went on a tourists' horseback trail ride into the dry, steep, brushy mountains. I gestured my hand to the countryside and asked our crusty guide, "Venado?", the Spanish word for deer.

"Si!" came his enthusiastic answer.

"Blanco (white)?" I asked, pointing to where a tail would be if I had one. His eyes got bigger, his smile wider: "Sí, sí — blanco cola (tail)!"

We were pleased to know that we both loved and lived with the same deer. Even with my limited Spanish and his limited English, we figured out that we both hunted venado. In fact, I suspect it was venado that we ate in fajitas back at the adobe ranch house after the trail ride.

Whitetails thrive everywhere because they are habitat generalists. Plop them down where there is some forage and a little cover or topography in which to hide, and they will make a go of it. You have to admire that toughness and adaptability.

WONDERS OF PERSONALITY

Scientists have identified dozens of whitetail subspecies. While specimens' body sizes differ greatly (compare a Florida or Mississippi buck to a bruiser of the same age in South Dakota, Iowa or Saskatchewan), a whitetail is a whitetail wherever you go.

That's what makes these deer so successful in so many places. All whitetails are masters of evasion. What other game

From North to South and East to West, buck or doe, big or small or in-between, a whitetail is a whitetail.

A whitetail can swivel each ear (with over 24 square inches of sound-catching surface area) in different directions to pinpoint noises.

animal exhibits such steely nerves? Evolution has eliminated panicky deer, and relegated us to hunt a race of wily, elusive, skulking hiders that can disappear while surviving below your very nose.

Once, in a Wisconsin woodlot, I jumped a group of does. They loped out across an alfalfa field, but stopped at some plowed ground and ran back into the woods.

I started sneaking toward them for a shot. At one point, as I ducked under a vine, my eyes met those of a buck — *three yards away!* Neck outstretched and chin on the ground, he leapt up when our eyes met, and dodged my flying slugs as he sped off unscathed.

That deer was not planning on moving an inch until my body language indicated I saw him. *That's* nerves! And it makes me wonder — how many other deer do we walk past at point blank range? We probably don't want to know.

WONDERS OF ATHLETICS

When a whitetail finally decides to move out, there is no hesitation or holding back. The show can run the gamut from sneaky to graceful to spectacular. Take some time to marvel at the next whitetail you see in motion.

A sneaking deer can tip-toe gingerly through "cornflake" leaves and not make a crackle, crunch or sound. These whitetails walk, almost comically, on the points of their hooves, to minimize the amount of surface area compressing the crunchiness. Dainty does and broad-shouldered bucks alike can move without making a noise.

The trot is the whitetail's most graceful gait. With head up and tail erect, the deer's legs move but the body seems to float across space. A trot eats up ground, but this middle-gear gait doesn't begin to kick the whitetail's athletic abilities into drive.

Full gear happens when a deer gallops: Two or three long strides followed by a bound that can cover up to 30 feet in itself.

Top speeds of 35 m.p.h. are possible. Few predators can hope to catch a healthy, galloping deer, and most won't even try.

But escape is not all about speed. Agility and leaping power also play into the whitetail's locomotion equation.

A deer can cut, veer and dodge through thick cover without losing stride. If you've ever butchered your own whitetail, you know why they can perform this feat: The front legs are not connected to the body via sockets, like how your arm is attached to your shoulder. Rather, the front legs are attached only by tendons and ligaments, and you can easily remove a leg from the deer's body with your pocket knife. Without joints, those front quarters shift and shimmy at will.

A whitetail's leaping power is unmatched. From a standing start, most whitetails can leap a six- to seven-foot barrier. With a little speed behind it, an eight- to nine-foot barrier is easily surmountable.

One day while we were eating lunch at our vehicles parked along a country road, a couple hunters started banging away down in the woods. We grabbed our guns as two does exited the timber and started running toward us. From the road, there wasn't much we could do but watch.

The whitetails soon hit full gear, approached our position, navigated the field fence without breaking stride, hit gravel, gathered, leaped over the trunk of my Uncle Alvin's 1965 Ford

Most nature whitetails can jump a six- to seven-foot-high barrier from a standing start, and clear eight to nine feet with a little run.

Galaxy 500, hit gravel again, and continued across the other fence. They crossed a field in split seconds, then were gone.

It was quite a show. One that only whitetails could put on.

WONDERS OF SENSES

Hiding and sneaking are a whitetail's preferred lines of defense. His athleticism will get him out of a pickle, but it is a deer's finely-honed and spectacularly acute senses of smell, hearing and sight that alert it to impending danger.

A whitetail's senses are so good, it is a wonder that we sensory-challenged humans ever kill a deer. Certainly, if we weren't armed with high-powered rifles, efficient slug guns, straight-shooting muzzleloaders or effective bows, few deer would make their way into hunters' hands. Modern-day hunting tools are the equalizers we inferior humans need against the deer's superior senses, to have any chance of bringing home some venison.

Smell is the whitetail's first line of sensory defense. A whitetail trusts his nose fully, and in many cases will rely solely on the information that the nose provides, without confirmation from another sense. Whitetails trust their noses like we humans do our eyes.

Next time you get a deer, study the size of those nostrils for sucking in air and scent. The snout is long for a reason: Hundreds of square inches of smelling tissue — folds upon folds of it — process air, collect information and send it to the whitetail's brain, where the space devoted to interpreting smells is large and highly developed.

While not as amazing as its sense of smell, a whitetail's hearing puts yours and mine to shame. A deer's ear offers about 24 square inches of surface area to gather sound. What's more, each ear operates independently of the other one, and is able to swivel, cup, twirl and rotate to pinpoint the source of specific sounds.

A whitetail's sight is merely good. But in one aspect, deer vision is spectacular: the eyes' ability to detect movement. Sit stone still and a deer won't recognize you. Make one little-bitty errant movement and you're pegged.

Evolution has sacrificed visual cones (which produce color and sharpness in images) in deer and replaced them with extra rods (for seeing well in the low light situations of dawn and dusk, the times of day when deer and predators are active). Those big bulging eyes also present a 300-degree range of vision — perfect for spotting sneaky predators.

A good whiff of a bad smell will put a deer on high alert — into deep hiding, or sneaking or running off. But an errant sound or visual suspicion usually needs a confirmation from another sense. That's why deer like to circle downwind of something they're uncomfortable with. The old hoof-stomp — where a deer thumps its hoof on the ground to surprise you into making a movement and giving up your position — relates to a whitetail's senses. It's one way to get a visual warning from something the deer sees or hears.

WONDERS OF THE HUNT

There was a time when simply *seeing* a deer made for a successful hunting season. And in the county where I grew up, you got your name in the paper, along with the hundred or so other lucky hunters, if you registered a deer. Shooting one, any deer, was a big deal.

These days, a couple thousand deer are registered there each fall. And it's not even a prime hunting destination. To shoot a doe is just business. A small or average buck doesn't command a second glance. Seeing or shooting a deer is not that big of a deal. The situation and feelings are the same in the other places I chase whitetails too. In some ways, it's too bad.

But in many ways, I like these "good new days" too. There's more opportunity to see and study deer, and more chances to hunt them. And that is, after all and without apologies, what we love to do most!

These are still the same deer we hunted way back when. It's just that now, there are more of them. And all the more need to appreciate all the wonders of each and every whitetail.

With its long snout housing fold upon fold of delicate smelling tissue — and a brain designed to interpret everything the nose is telling it — a whitetail uses and trusts its sense of smell more than any other sense.

Little States, Big Bucks

JACK RODGERS

You might be surprised at the caliber of the whitetails living along the heavily-populated East Coast.

They're going to hate me for telling you this. I thought it was a helluva big buck. My friend just sat next to it, shaking. The inside spread was just short of 20 inches, and the longest of the 11 tines was ten inches. The base of the antlers was as big around as a baseball bat handle. But it was something that our host said that really got our attention.

"Son, that's a nice one," he said to my buddy as we rattled down the farm lane in his battered pickup. "But at least you didn't shoot the big one. I'd like my boy to get a chance at him." Big one?!

A CASE STUDY: DELAWARE

They've kept the secret very well so far, these Delaware deer hunters. Quietly they let the larger deer factories crow about projected harvests. They smile when they hear stories from va-

cationers about "the big eight-point I shot back home." Then in November, they thrash around in some forsaken swamp or thicket, squint down the barrel of their shotguns and drag out some gosh-awful big buck. It happens every fall.

Hunters primarily think of Delaware as a premier waterfowling destination. That reputation is certainly well deserved. However, increasing numbers of hunters are taking advantage of the Diamond State's expanding whitetail herd.

The increased interest in deer hunting likely stems from the fact that nearly 10 percent of Delaware's land mass is state owned and open for public hunting. Throughout the 1970s and '80s, Delaware posted annual deer harvests of around 5,000 whitetails. Today, hunters take home nearly 14,000 deer annually.

But that's not all. These Diamond State deer are healthy. The average weight of a field-dressed yearling buck from Delaware's poorest deer area was recently calculated at 110 pounds. That is, incidentally, a whopping 30 pounds heavier than the average dressed weight of yearling bucks in some of the better known deer states. The largest Delaware bucks taken each year dress more than 200 pounds. In fact, bucks tipping the scales at 240 pounds have been taken.

Another method used to evaluate the overall health of the

▰▰▰

"Delaware hunters are highly selective in terms of waiting for a buck, particularly early in the season."

▰▰▰

herd is the development of antlers among yearling bucks. Recent harvest statistics indicate that only 13 percent of yearling bucks taken are spikes. Again, this figure compares very favorably to states like Pennsylvania, New York and Wisconsin. It's no wonder that wildlife managers have had difficulty getting hunters to harvest more does.

In fact, the antlerless harvest usually comes in around 40 percent even though hunters are allowed two deer of either sex with their regular tags and can purchase additional antlerless permits.

"Our hunters are highly selective in terms of waiting for a buck, particularly early in the season," says Lloyd Alexander of the Delaware Division of Natural Resources. "And they have good reason to be. We have some outstanding animals, with bucks of ten or more points being taken from every part of the state." Alexander believes that the combination of better nutrition coupled with less stress than higher harvest/higher

hunter participation states accounts for the heavier Diamond State bucks. "And," he added with a laugh, "as for the racks, there is no comparison."

Most dedicated trophy chasers know that several conditions need exist in order to grow superior animals — genetics, good nutrition and sanctuaries that allow bucks to live at least three or four years. Delaware is rich with country that offers all three ingredients. To find them, hunters need only start their search by looking west.

After a devastating ice storm hammered many woodlots along the state's western border, virtually every tree lost limbs and tops, and much of the state's forested areas were covered with deadfall and brush. This cover not only helped hide whitetails, but severely restricted hunter mobility. Whitetails consequently had a greater likelihood of living long enough to grow antlers of record-book proportions.

"Zones in the western edge of the state along the Maryland border are great areas for heavy animals," Alexander says.

A woodlot in this part of the state that a friend and I hunt illustrates the potential of the region.

The lot is large and contains a great deal of brush and heavy cover. The deer in our block could easily dodge around us (though two didn't) or sneak out onto adjacent areas closed to hunting. There is virtually no hunting pressure in surrounding sections. On the opening day of the season last year, my friend and I saw only two other hunters along the road. One had a fat doe, and his partner had taken a 170-pound ten-point. He had also seen a larger buck; one he called "magnificent." Other than this pair of hunters, you wouldn't have known that the season was open.

Looking at the general lack of hunting pressure, difficult terrain and nearby sanctuary areas, one can easily imagine these bucks surviving to reach trophy age. My friend has taken two 11-point bucks dressing more than 190 pounds from this

Fine bucks by any standard that came from states not recognized for whitetails.

Bowhunters in states like Delaware have excellent opportunities to pursue bucks that are sometimes unpressured.

western border area during the last few years. Both sported inside spreads of approximately 20 inches.

But the western edge of the state is not the only locale where the bruisers live. The coastal edges of Delaware also provide realistic opportunities to take a big buck. Shorebound vacationers zooming through this area are often treated to scenery including heavy-antlered bucks and groups of does standing around soybean fields. Frequently, these seemingly unsophisticated coastal whitetails pull such stunts during the middle of sultry summer days, causing northern tourists to scratch their heads in disbelief. Veteran Delaware whitetail enthusiasts know better and are aware that there are few sure things when hunting these adaptive creatures. This area, summertime appearances notwithstanding, presents its own unique challenges.

The coastal deer, like whitetails everywhere, quickly abandon their normal routine when subjected to human intrusion. The deer react to pressure by leaving their normal haunts and hiding out in vast stretches of marsh. In such places, every high spot becomes a haven for deer. Few hunters slog their way out onto such "ground," and those that do rarely return. The deer merely wait it out during daylight hours, then slip back to the fields at night to contribute to the headaches of local farmers. Daylight hunting season visits to such fields often leave Delaware deer hunters surrounded by a multitude of tracks and an amazing lack of live deer. These whitetails, having learned to play the game, have a far greater chance of being killed by a car

than shot by a hunter. Again, a fair share of coastal bucks live to old age and grow trophy antlers.

Despite the challenges presented by the geography, Delaware's coastal bucks are not unhuntable. One strategy might be to center around the early archery and muzzleloader opportunities that the state provides. The archery season opens on September 1 (excepting a Sunday) and the six-day early muzzleloader season is held in early October. Though the ranks of participants in both sports increase yearly, the early seasons offer advantages to trophy hunters. Whitetails are generally less pressured during these seasons and consequently still in patterns of daylight movement.

As noted before, a serious problem facing hunters along the coast is the quick conversion of wary bucks to a nocturnal lifestyle. While these coastal marshes do present a challenge to any deer hunter, whitetails using such areas have a chink in their armor. Water.

In many cases, there will be some water areas, be they streams, rivers or standing ponds, that funnel the deer using the marshes as a sanctuary. The deer might not want to cross them due to depth, bottom content or other factors, but most wetlands feature these funnel areas. A friend and I found one typical location before last November's shotgun season opened.

A tidal river separated lush agricultural fields from an island of small trees and brush out on the open marsh. The deer were using the island as a sanctuary area. We found a finger of brush leading from the fields to the river. Across the river was another short stretch of brush that led to the island. It seemed the perfect spot for the deer to cross the river during legal shooting hours. We helped friend and NAHC Member Mark Wells erect a treestand on this spot, and he killed a 165-pound eight-point within minutes after the season opened. There are lots of similar locations out there. It just takes legwork to find them.

OTHER STATES

Hunters looking for a big buck in a small state have other options besides Delaware. Like Delaware, Maryland boasts a storied tradition as a waterfowling area. But according to Tom Mathews of the Maryland Department of Fish and Game, The Free State promises some fine deer hunting as well.

According to Mathews, Maryland offers great diversity in terms of whitetail habitat, from the Piedmont zone to the coastal plains. Hunters can take advantage of a variety of season types stretching from September 15 to the end of January. Bag limits are also liberal. Mathews points out that sportsmen are able to harvest a single deer with a firearm, bow and muzzleloader, respectively. Maryland deer hunters can also profit by taking advantage of bonus plans and harvest additional deer by season. But quantity is not all that Maryland's whitetail herd has to offer. There are some record-class bucks out there trying to win over the hearts of the state's waterfowlers.

Mathews concedes that there are some regions of the state more likely to produce bigger bucks than others. Check out Kent and Dorcester counties, he says. But Mathews is also quick to point out that heavyweight whitetails are also increasingly utilizing suburban communities as refuge areas. These deer can live to the ripe old age needed to reach trophy size, so hunters interested in a bragging rack might check out some of the locations fringing metropolitan areas within the state.

Another small state that is producing more and more quality experiences for deer hunters is New Jersey. The Garden State offers six different seasons totaling 105 days of deer hunting, and there are some bruisers available here, too. According to Dan Ferrigno with the state Wildlife Commission, good bucks are found all throughout the state.

Ferrigno noted several counties that have a good track record for producing 200-pound bucks. Gloucester, Mercer, Salem and Monmouth counties (particularly western Monmouth) were all on his list. But, like Delaware, the coastal regions should be scouted thoroughly.

"The deer are smart," Ferrigno says. "They take advantage of high spots and dense Phragmites stands. After they get in there, there's not much you can do." Combine such conditions with available agricultural crops for nutrition, and the table is set for trophy potential.

Ferrigno has one more tip for Garden State hunters seeking a big buck: Hunt early.

"Archers take a majority of our 200-pound bucks," he says. "Our firearms seasons are held after the rut. Bucks have expended a great deal of energy during that period, and so they weigh less."

Deer hunting for most of us will always evoke certain familiar images. For many, the visions of trackless wilderness, the heft of a familiar rifle and the carnival atmosphere of Opening Day are all integral parts of the experience.

While there is some of this in these small states, there is a great deal of a quieter, different type of hunting. There are places where you can count the shots on opening day on your fingers. You can even find a place to park. You might see more brushpiles than deer, or swat more mosquitoes than you release arrows. But, then again, you just might find out why some of these small states are so special to whitetail hunters.

You might be standing in the dark with a buck in the bed of your pickup. The farmer might congratulate you and tell you of an even bigger one he saw that summer. And as you look out there in the darkness, you know that in some forgotten corner of these diamonds in the rough, there just could be.

Biggest of the Little

Northeastern deer hunters used to have to travel to the Midwest, Texas or Canada to have a chance at seeing a record-class buck. Not any more. Here are just a handful of the giant northeastern whitetails taken in the past few years.

DELAWARE

Hunter: Robert Reeves Jr.
Score: 197 typical
Location: Kent County

MARYLAND

Hunter: Bill Crutchfield Jr.
Score: 268 nontypical
Location: Charles County

NEW JERSEY

Hunter: Joseph Meglio
Score: 192 nontypical
Location: Monmouth County

NEW HAMPSHIRE

Hunter: John Klucky
Score: 199 5/8 (nontypical)
Location: Merrimack County

Blue-Collar Book Bucks

GLENN SAPIR

NAHC Member Mike Chirico with some of his best whitetails.

WHITETAIL WISDOM

When a hunter etches his name in the record books six times, you might draw certain conclusions. You might imagine a free-spender devoting significant resources to hiring the best professional guides and outfitters in renowned destinations, such as Saskatchewan and Texas. You probably picture a tense, call it "obsessive," determination to become immortalized in hunting archives. Quite likely you'd conjure up an image of a young athlete, physically equipped to meet the rigors that the special stresses of big buck hunting present.

Enter Mike Chirico, a New York resident and a member of the North American Hunting Club. Chirico has bagged many bucks with his bow, shotgun and muzzleloader, including a half-dozen that have received record-book recognition. Four of them have been included in the New York State Big Bucks Club record book; four have garnered archery's Pope and Young Club recognition; and one earned a place in both the Boone and Crockett Club and the National Muzzle Loading Association's Long Hunter Society archives.

Chirico hasn't traveled across the continent to buy the best opportunities for trophy bucks. In fact, four of his six giants have been taken within a half-hour of his home, Buchanan, New York — a suburb on the Hudson River some 40 miles north of the Big Apple. The other two, including the Boone and Crockett and Long Hunter Society monster, were shot on a Maryland farm on the Eastern Shore.

Chirico could hardly be called a young athlete. Though physically fit, he still says, "I like to hunt with my son — not only for his company, but to help drag out the deer."

DEDICATION EQUALS SUCCESS

Though Chirico is an avid deer hunter, calling him "obsessed" would be unfair. Instead, you could describe Mike Chirico as a dedicated deer hunter, intent on harvesting big bucks. He works for his deer — before the season in preparation and during the season with hunting know-how. Chirico hasn't come up with any truly revolutionary techniques. He's simply a blue-collar hunter whose hard-work ethic pays off. I guess you could call him an Everyman's role model, and no doubt you could learn something from him.

Ask him to what he attributes his success, and he'll tell you in his typical modest demeanor:

"Thirty-nine years of mistakes."

After the chuckling subsides, in a more serious moment, he'll tell you it's "being in the right place at the right time." How does he maximize the chance of "being in the right place at the right time?"

"Practicing is the key," says Chirico.

There is no "right time," if you aren't prepared to make the shot when it presents itself.

Because bowhunting is the only legal form of deer hunting in Westchester, his home county, that is the sport to which he devotes most of his attention. He practices religiously at a 3-D range, and has set up a target in his backyard.

"Whenever I can fit it in, I am practicing," the hunter says. "There's nothing more important to success! You have to know

Bowhunting is Mike's bread and butter and the method he's used to tag most of his record-class bucks.

when to release your arrow on the different shots, such as quartering away and broadside."

ACCESS IS THE FIRST KEY

Another important preseason activity is locating land and securing permission to hunt. In Westchester County, not an acre of public land is open to hunting. So, Chirico must look to private landowners as his key to access. In affluent, suburban northern Westchester County, huntable tracts are usually estates of five acres or more.

"I'll drive the roads, keeping my eyes open," Chirico says. "I'll look for yards that have deer fences. In the winter I'll search for landscaping that is protected by burlap. I'll keep my eyes open for an evident browse line on someone's trees."

Not only does he keep his eyes open, his ears are permanently attuned to opportunities.

"I am always listening, whether I am waiting in line at a delicatessen or mingling at a house party. When a guy says, 'The deer are eating me out of house and home,' I'm ready to come to his rescue."

But there's more to it than that:

"In suburban areas, you must get a landowner's trust and respect. My keys are a handshake, an introduction and credentials.

Mike Chirico's Record-Book Bucks

B&C Score	Points	Dressed Weight	Where Taken	Record Book(s)
160⅜	8	215	Maryland	Boone and Crockett Long Hunter Society
153⅜	10	160	Westchester	Pope and Young New York Big Bucks
140⅛	10	165	Westchester	Pope and Young New York Big Bucks
138⅛	10	150	Maryland	Pope and Young
134⅜	9	130	Westchester	Pope and Young New York Big Bucks
122⅜	8	160	Westchester	New York Big Bucks
120⅝	8	170	Westchester	New York Big Bucks

I like to emphasize that I have been a New York state bowhunter education instructor since the program's inception and a North American Hunting Club member. That often seems to mean a lot."

The right contacts can include people other than landowners. Chirico, for example, has long been an active member of the Westchester County Bowhunters Association.

"By going to meetings and making friends, I've come to learn about hunting opportunities in the area that I wouldn't have otherwise," he said.

SCOUTING IS A MUST

Of course, scouting the land to which he has access is another essential part of Chirico's hunting preparation.

"I've taken ten white-tailed bucks from the same tree on a four-acre parcel. I know where the bucks travel in that woodlot." What does he look for when scouting?

"There are three main ways I can identify whether an area is holding a big buck," Chirico explains. "Everyone knows to look for scrapes. Well, I look for big scrapes. I've seen them the size of a kitchen tabletop or a car hood. When you see one that size, you can bet you are dealing with a very big-bodied deer. You can't be sure that it's wearing a record-book rack, but it's likely a wall-hanger.

"The second sign is rubs. Again, everyone knows rubs are a sign of bucks. But what I'm looking for are rubs not only on saplings, but on bigger trees. When you find a 10-inch-diameter tree that has been rubbed, a trophy is in the woods.

"Third, I put time in just watching. I like to find high spots, take a ground stand before the season, and just watch, becoming, like the animal I am going to hunt, aware of everything

around me. That way I'll often make a sighting of the big bucks I will later hunt."

"I'm a firm believer in high spots—small ridges and knolls," he says. "From there deer can wind danger, and see and hear everything. That's where the big bucks are most comfortable."

His theory reminds me of Tom Mosher, a remarkably successful deer hunting outfitter in New Brunswick who had long ago espoused to me his belief in "rutting knolls," elevated pieces of land where big bucks in rut would travel. When exploring new hunting areas, Mosher studies topographical maps, looking for elevated ground in swamps and marshes, and if they check out, that is often where he sets up his treestands.

In Maryland, Chirico's hunting takes place in hardwood lots adjoining soybean and cornfields and marshes on the land that he leases with several other hunters.

In either case, treestands are an essential part of his hunting strategy, and treestand placement is vital to success.

"I always try to set up so that I am downwind of where I think the big buck is going to be," Chirico says. "I'm also always aware of the background. In Westchester, for instance, the bow season runs from November 1 through all of December. So, for the whole season, the trees are bare, and don't kid yourself; deer look up. If I'm silhouetted against a bare skyline, they'll see me."

Instead, Chirico looks for stands of trees that will conceal his shape, like hemlocks or other evergreens.

"One year I took a seven-pointer with the bow," Chirico says. "It wasn't a record-book buck, but it was a nice one. It had seen me in the morning, but that same day I went home for lunch, cut down a branch from a pin oak that still had its dead, brown leaves, and I brought the branch up to my stand. I wired it to the tree behind me—and killed that seven-pointer that afternoon, from the same stand he had spotted me in that morning!"

TAKE CARE OF DETAILS

It's apparent that Chirico not only pays attention to the basics, but is willing to do the little extras necessary to get the big buck. Chirico believes it is important to allow at least a half-hour for the woods to settle down, so he always gets set up early.

"Typically, I will drive to a hunting spot near home and get in the woods a half-hour to 45 minutes before light. I'll pack in my portable treestand, and I'll pack my one-piece insulated suit in the stand. After the average walk of a quarter mile to my tree, I'll put on my suit, get my safety belt on, and get set up."

That's the scenario that starts most of Mike's hunts, and it is the one that began this one. The day before, Mike had collected an eight-pointer with his 60-pound Hoyt bow, so on this morning he told his friend and his son, with whom he was hunting, that he would only take a nine-point or better.

Mike let four young bucks walk, living up to his promise.

"Besides, if you really want to get a big buck, you have to let the smaller ones go by," Chirico insists. "That sounds simple enough, and most hunters know it, but most shoot anyway at the first buck that they see!"

"In sight of my son, a big buck came over a knoll. It presented me with a shot, and I took it. The buck went 60 yards and died. The arrow had gone through its lungs. It turned out to be a ten-pointer, measuring 140⅛ and weighing 165 pounds dressed."

Though his lifetime home of Westchester is from where three of his Pope and Young bucks have come, it was in Maryland that the bruiser that simultaneously got him into the Boone and Crockett Club and Long Hunter Society annals lived and died. It was a special three-day blackpowder hunt falling between bow and gun seasons during late October.

"I made my quarter-mile hike to a holly tree in a hardwood forest next to a marsh," Chirico says. "In early morning three small bucks came by. I let them go. Then I heard a stick crack behind me. I turned to see what looked like a good-sized buck some 60 yards away. I aimed my .50 caliber Thompson/ Center and fired. The buck ran 70 yards, out of sight."

"I waited three-quarters of an hour, then tracked him," he says. "When I saw him, I couldn't believe his size! The typical eight-point buck later scaled 215 pounds dressed and measured 160⅜ B&C points."

That hunt typified the basics, along with the extras, that Chirico brings to every one of his whitetail hunts. He had scouted the area, situated his treestand accordingly and planned his strategy. He let three bucks go by, then relied on the aim much practice had honed.

Maryland is not a renowned deer hunting state. But he was in the right place at the right time, and put his 39 years of learning from his mistakes to work. That day in October Mike Chirico did what any one of us might do if we are willing to follow some of the same rules this fellow NAHC member has carved for himself.

One of Mike's best bucks is this blackpowder beauty he shot in Maryland.

Deer Camp Quiz

CHARLES J. ALSHEIMER

Each year, North American Hunting Club members gather in tents, cabins, campers and houses from Pennsylvania to Texas and Florida to Saskatchewan to celebrate a sport rich with tradition.

Deer season.

No matter what your deer camp looks like or where it's found across the whitetail's range, these precious days are tough to top with any other hunting adventure. But if you ask almost any deer hunter why deer camp and deer season are so important, his or her answer probably won't focus on tagging a whitetail. In fact, that might not be part of the answer at all. Instead, you're likely to hear about the camaraderie and fellowship unique to the deer woods and deer camps.

That might mean a friendly card game or stories from the day's hunt. It probably sometimes involves some lively discussion about the matters of deer hunting, deer behavior and deer biology. Well, we've decided to provide more fodder for your deer camp conversations this fall. And we hope you take this book along with you so that your buddies can also take our "Deer Camp Quiz." You can find the answers after the quiz. Loser has to wash the dishes!

Good luck.

1. Which whitetail gland is considered the "rut" gland?

A. metatarsal
B. tarsal
C. nasal
D. none of the above

2. When a white-tailed buck works a scrape's overhanging licking branch, which gland(s) does he rub on the branch to leave his scent?

A. preorbital gland
B. forehead gland
C. metatarsal gland
D. both A and B
E. none of the above

3. In the North, the velvet covering a whitetail's antlers is shed during what period of time?

A. end of July, early August
B. end of August, early September
C. the first of October
D. none of the above

4. During the scrape-making process, a white-tailed buck urinates over which gland to leave scent?

A. metatarsal
B. preorbital
C. tarsal
D. nasal

5. A whitetail literally lives and dies by which of its senses?

A. hearing
B. eyesight
C. smell
D. none of the above

6. The largest known whitetail buck killed in North America weighed how much after its entrails were removed?

A. 310 pounds
B. 355 pounds
C. 402 pounds
D. 431 pounds

7. What is the minimum score for entry into the whitetail typical category of the Boone and Crockett Club's all-time record book?

A. 150
B. 160
C. 170
D. 195

8. Just prior to and during the rut, what weather condition causes deer to be active?

A. a heavy snow
B. a rapidly falling or rising barometer
C. a heavy rain storm
D. none of the above

9. Which whitetail scrape is considered the most productive for hunters during the rut?

    A. boundary scrape
    B. secondary scrape
    C. primary scrape
    D. all of the above

10. What is the most important physical aspect of a whitetail's scrape?

A. that it be located on level ground
B. that it can be easily seen by other deer
C. that it has a good licking branch above it
D. all of the above

11. When hunting on the side of a hill, which way do the thermals move early in the morning?

A. sideways
B. downhill
C. uphill
D. Thermals can't be predicted

12. When there is a steady breeze blowing, wind currents are the most difficult to predict in which area?

A. in the bottom of a ravine
B. in flat woods
C. on a sidehill
D. in rolling country

13. Whitetail rubs made on trees 5 to 6 inches in diameter were made by what bucks?

A. spike bucks
B. 2-year-old bucks
C. trophy-sized mature bucks
D. both B and C
E. all of the above

14. The majority of white-tailed bucks killed by hunters are how old?

A. 1½ years old
B. 2½ years old
C. 3½ years old
D. more than 5 years old

15. When a white-tailed doe comes into estrus, what does it signal?

A. It's about to give birth.
B. It's ready to breed.
C. It'll run from bucks.
D. It'll respond to antler rattling.

16. In a national survey, it was determined that the average treestand height among America's bowhunters is:

A. 10 feet
B. 30 feet
C. 15 to 16 feet
D. 25 feet

17. When is the best time to imitate antler rattling to attract white-tailed bucks?

A. during the two-week period just prior to the does coming into estrus
B. during the breeding time
C. in early September
D. in late December

18. During the rattling sequence, if a buck hangs up just out of range what can be done to bring the buck closer?

A. keep on rattling
B. move to another spot and rattle again
C. make a couple of soft grunts on a grunt tube
D. all of the above

19. For ranges out to 250 yards, which calibers and bullet weights are best for deer hunters?

A. .243 Win. with a 75-grain bullet
B. .270 Win. with a 130-grain bullet
C. .30-06 with a 150-grain bullet
D. 12 gauge shotgun slug
E. all of the above
F. both B and C

20. A forkhorn, crotch horn or Y-buck has how many total points?

A. two
B. six
C. four
D. none of the above

21. During the early fall, which will respond best to a fawn bleat call?

A. fawn
B. doe
C. buck

22. Where is one of the best places to hang a treestand and hunt whitetails during the rut?

A. along the edge of a field
B. in deep forest settings
C. near a highway crossing
D. in a natural funnel area between a favorite food source and bedding area

23. During late-winter scouting forays, what should your goal be?

A. find heavy concentrations of deer sign
B. locate the primary bedding area
C. look for possible stand locations for the coming season
D. determine if any of the old scrapes have been used since the season ended
E. all of the above

24. For an evening sit during September and early October, where will be the best place to hang a treestand if you find large rubs and scrapes around the edges of a clover field?

A. approximately 75 yards into the woods on the downwind side of two well-used intersecting trails
B. on the downwind side of where a well-used trail enters the field
C. near the biggest rubs
D. downwind of the largest scrape along the field's edge

25. When a full moon occurs during the chase phase of the rut, the best time to hunt is:

A. dawn
B. dusk
C. mid-day
D. all of the above

26. During a heavy snowstorm, the best hunting strategy is:

A. treestand hunting
B. still-hunting
C. rattling
D. none of the above

27. When scouting during the early autumn months, the most reliable buck sign you will find is what?

A. dense deer droppings in feeding area
B. well-used deer trails
C. rubs on trees 4 to 6 inches in diameter
D. fresh scrapes
E. both C and D

28. What is the best way to find a nocturnal buck during the rut?

A. hunting in known feeding areas
B. hunting as close as you can to bedding areas, downwind of trails
C. hunting in the bedding area
D. all of the above

29. Once the breeding begins, the best hunting tactic is:

A. begin hunting the doe groups
B. continue to hunt the scrape lines you've been hunting
C. try rattling throughout the day
D. all of the above

30. When hunting apple orchards during the pre-rut in late September and early October, it is best to hang your treestand where?

A. in the tree that has the most fruit hanging on the branches
B. in the middle of the orchard
C. downwind of the most active trail that enters the orchard
D. none of the above

31. When checking for tracks in scrapes during the rut, how wide would a whitetail track have to be (minimum width) for it to be made by a mature buck?

A. 1 inch wide
B. 2 inches wide
C. 2¼ inches wide
D. 3 inches wide

32. When bowhunting over a doe decoy during the rut, the best setup will be in which of the following locations?

A. in an open travel corridor between the bedding and feeding area
B. along the edge of a clover field
C. in a thick bedding area
D. none of the above

Quiz Answers

1. B. tarsal

2. D. When working the licking branch a whitetail buck rubs its preorbital and forehead gland on the branch to leave as much of his scent as possible.

3. B. end of August, early September

4. C. During this process a buck's urine passes over his tarsal gland and into the pawed-out surface of a scrape, leaving the buck's distinctive odor for other deer to smell.

5. C. A whitetail's sense of smell is its greatest asset and the most finely tuned sense it has.

6. D. This buck fell to bowhunter John Annett of Ontario, Canada, in 1977. It dressed out at 431 pounds on government-certified scales.

7. C. 170

8. B. When the barometric pressure moves rapidly in either direction, whitetails will be on the move to favorite feeding sources.

9. C. A primary scrape is used by many different bucks and is often referred to as a "whitetail bus station."

10. C. Without an adequate licking branch, scrapes will seldom be reused.

11. C. In the morning, thermals will move uphill as the temperature rises.

12. A. One of the most difficult areas to predict wind current is in the bottom of a ravine, regardless of how hard the wind is blowing. In these places, air currents constantly eddy back and forth.

13. D. both B and C. Any buck 2 years of age or older is capable of making rubs on trees this size. Spikes will seldom, if ever, make a substantial rub on a tree this large. Instead, they make small rubs on finger-size saplings.

14. A. 1½-year-old yearlings. In many northern states, more than 70 percent of the gun harvests are made up of this age class.

15. B. The doe is ready to stand and be bred by a buck. Does will be in estrus for roughly 24 hours, and if not bred during this time will come into estrus again in approximately 29 days.

16. C. 15 to 16 feet high

17. A. The two-week "window" just before the breeding time is the best time to rattle in and kill a whitetail buck. During this period, a buck's aggression level is highest. He's constantly on the move and is making many scrapes and rubs. Once the breeding begins, he can still be rattled into range, but it will be more difficult.

18. C. When a whitetail buck hangs up and will not come any closer, it's because he's apprehensive or can't see the two fighting bucks. Because he is usually quite close when this happens, it's not advisable to rattle anymore since you might spook him. Rather, rely on a grunt tube to bring the buck closer. Usually it only takes one or two guttural grunts to bring the buck within shooting range when this happens.

19. F. both B and C. When thinking of whitetail hunting loads and calibers, remember that (as a rule of thumb) the bullet should have at least 1,200 foot-pounds of energy at the point of impact for ample killing power. Because the 75-grain .243 Win. and 12 gauge fall way short of this at ranges out to 250 yards, only the .270 Win. and .30-06 in this list are adequate.

20. C. four

21. B. During the early fall, does will respond well to a fawn bleat call.

22. D. Funnel areas are great locations to hunt whitetails and excellent places to intercept an elusive buck during the rut.

23. E. All of this information can be gathered in winter and used the following season.

24. A. During the pre-rut period, most bucks, especially mature bucks, don't move into a field to feed until dark. By hanging a stand inside the woods where two trails intersect, you'll be able to intercept a buck as it heads for the field during the last minutes of daylight.

25. D. This is a tough one. Most hunters would probably pick answer C. However, after years of observation (with camera and hunting tool), the clear answer is all three when bucks are chasing does during the rut. I've killed my biggest bucks and taken my best photographs by hunting throughout the day when the full moon falls during this time.

26. B. There is no better time to still-hunt whitetails than during a snowstorm. The snow not only muffles your sound but also makes it tougher for deer to see you.

27. E. While droppings and tracks are sure deer sign, rubs and scrapes are positive indicators of the presence of bucks.

28. B. By getting as close as possible to the bedding area, you'll have a better chance of killing a nocturnal buck as it moves between the bedding and feeding areas. Hunting in the bedding area is a last-resort tactic. It can work, but more often than not spooks the buck, forcing him to take refuge in another location.

29. A. Once the breeding begins, nearly every hot doe has a buck in her thicket. Because of this, scraping activity drops off rapidly as the bucks change their daily habits. By hunting the known doe groups, your chances for success will soar during the breeding period.

30. C. Because one never knows which way a buck will go in a fruit-laden orchard, it's best to intercept him before he gets to the orchard and turns off in different directions.

31. C. Extensive research has shown that the width of a buck's track is a better indicator of the size of the animal than track length. Based on this research, bucks with a dressed weight of 170 to 190 pounds will almost always have a minimum track width of 2¼ inches.

32. A. During the rut, decoys work very well in a travel corridor between the bedding and feeding areas. The important thing is that the cover not be too thick or else the buck might not see the decoy. When using a doe decoy, try to position it 20 to 25 yards upwind of your stand.

Search for the Perfect Deer Camp

GREGG GUTSCHOW

Opening Day's best hours were gone. Shooting time closed a few hours ago and eight hunters with full bellies fought to stay awake as the cabin became too warm for long johns and flannel shirts. Only Dad's forkhorn buck hung outside in the starry darkness. It was a quiet day as Wisconsin openers go.

We'd seen good years and bad since we started our camp here many years ago. During the lean years, we'd argue the deer management strategies of the Department of Natural Resources. As armchair biologists, we'd decide in minutes why there weren't

enough deer or enough old bucks. And we'd talk about territories we'd heard of where trophy whitetails ran every ridge and slept in every swamp. Someday we ought to hunt there, someone would suggest. But that's as far as we ever strayed from our deer camp. Instead, another log crackled on the fire, and heavy eyes closed to dreams of a new day and an old stand.

We always return to that place, and I'm glad we do. With Opening Day on the horizon, that cozy cabin with the forest all around it seems like the most inviting place on Earth.

The quality of a deer camp, you see, is difficult to measure. Deer Camp could be a farmhouse, a tent, a log cabin or a camper-trailer. It could be in the middle of a forest or a field. It could consist of 10 hunters or two. Camaraderie? . . . Kind of. Male bonding? . . . Maybe. But it's much more.

It's the other hunters in camp; the memories; the anticipation; the handshakes; the deer tracks by your stand; the rifle you killed your first deer with; the knife your dad gave you; the respect for old bucks and older hunters. And still more. Much more. Deer Camp is certainly about simple pleasures like lantern light, a friendly card game and a warm sleeping bag. The necessary ingredients in the makings of a quality Deer Camp, however, are more complex. Deer Camp should make us better people. It should heighten our awareness of life in the wild. It should inspire the realization that in order to take, we all must be willing to give back. It should be a place where children learn lessons that they can not be taught in a classroom.

For youngsters fortunate enough to be raised in hunting families, Deer Camp is the grail. And if Deer Camp is as it should be, the place burns a vivid image into the soul of that young hunter. And as the years go by, the right deer camp makes old hunters afraid to die anywhere else.

Hunters who attempt to explain the significance of Deer Camp to others quickly realize that the endeavor is folly. The motive is a good one, though: If only nonhunters could truly appreciate the many rewards of Deer Camp, they then could certainly understand why we hunt. Maybe that's why so many have attempted to put words to this humble place. We'd like everyone to experience. To appreciate. To understand.

Who could love a place where snoring men cause frail walls to tremble; where the pungent odor of sweaty, wet wool socks drying by the wood stove permeates the air; where the toilet is 27 paces from the back door? Only a deer hunter.

If it's difficult to leave Deer Camp at the end of this season — if you have spent some of the best days of your life here — you have found the right place.

Count your blessings. And stay put.

First Deer

JOHN SLOAN

The boy awoke early. It wasn't surprising that he was up before the alarm went off. He had been so excited about his first deer hunt that he hadn't slept much all night.

He pulled on his long johns and wool socks and padded to the kitchen. His father was sitting at the table, obviously working on his second helping of coffee and biscuits.

The boy poured a glass of milk and quickly buttered four biscuits. He knew that he'd have trouble eating; he wanted to go hunting. His father blew across his coffee cup and smiled.

"You ready, Son? It's going to be a great day. We had a touch of frost last night. That's always good for deer hunting; gets them up and moving with first light," he said.

The boy was more than ready. All night he had been going over everything that he had learned in hunter education, and most of the night he had been seeing huge bucks with wide racks.

"Go on and get finished dressing," his father said. "It's time we were heading for the woods. It'll be light in an hour."

The boy quickly finished dressing, but paid special attention to tying his new hunting boots. He checked to make sure that he had his orange vest and hat and a box of cartridges for the old Winchester.

As he came into the kitchen, his father was casing the battered and scarred Model 94. "This is your rifle now, Son," he said. "It'd do well for you to keep in mind that you have to handle it safely and responsibly or I'll have to take it away from you until you're old enough to treat it with respect."

"Yes sir," the boy said. "I'll take real good care of it and clean it every day, and I'll be real careful with it, too."

As the man and boy left the house and climbed into the old hunting truck, there was still no sign of light in the sky. The boy knew that they were going to a piece of private property that belonged to one of his fa-

ther's friends. His father had been scouting and bowhunting there quite a bit the last two weeks. The boy felt sure that his father had seen a lot of deer there, although he had not said so.

The old heater clattered and whined and just barely put a feeble trickle of warm air around their feet as they drove down the winding blacktop road. The boy dreamed of a buck. His dad had told him that it would be fine, even good if he killed a doe for his first deer. But no 13-year-old dreams of shooting a doe.

His father finally swung the truck off the hard road onto a gravel track that led to an abandoned farm house. He stopped in front of the locked gate and parked under a giant maple tree.

The boy knew that they were the only ones who had permission to hunt here, and the gate, covered with posted signs, reassured him that he would be alone.

"Son, it's pretty cold this morning, but the walk up the ridge will warm you right away. I don't want you to put on your jacket until you get to your tree. That way you won't be all sweaty when you climb up. Be sure you have your orange on, and take this flashlight. Make sure your rifle is unloaded and follow right behind me. We'll try to slip in quietly."

The boy slung the rifle, and his father took the climbing treestand. They began the climb up the timbered ridge. He tried to walk quietly, but it seemed that every step was on a twig or dry leaf.

At the top of the ridge, his father swung a few yards left and stopped next to an old fence that was down in several places. "Listen close," his father whispered, "I know you know how to

Whether you're young, old or somewhere in between, the dream is the same. A sight like this. A buck like this. Just once.

use the climbing stand, and I've checked it to make sure that it is A-okay. I don't want you to go over 10 to 12 feet high. That's plenty high enough to see well, and it's more important to sit still. Here is your safety belt and your haul line. I'll put the stand on the tree and get you started."

The boy nodded even though he knew that his father couldn't see him in the dark. He had been practicing with the stand on a tree in the backyard and felt comfortable using it. He had also shot more than five boxes of ammunition through the gun at the range and could put five shots through an eight-inch circle at 100 yards. He knew how to load the rifle and handle it safely.

His dad quickly hung the stand and seat climber on a straight white oak on the edge of a cedar thicket. "This is it, Son," he said, "I've been watching deer here for three weeks. They come out of the cedars and feed under those oaks yonder. You'll be able to see the trees as soon as it gets light. It's about 50 yards to the edge of the cedars and 40 to the oaks. You should be in good shape to shoot from here.

"I want you to face toward those cedars; just where they point out. The deer will probably show up at that spot, but you keep your eyes peeled in all directions. Just turn your head slowly from time to time. And try not to fidget in your stand. Sit still.

■ ■ ■

"The man squeezed the boy's shoulder. 'Remember, Son, killing a deer isn't the most important thing this morning. Enjoy the woods and learn from them.' He resisted the urge to hug his son, turned and faded into the graying darkness."

■ ■ ■

"If you see a deer, don't jump up and start shooting. Pick a spot and take your time. Try to raise the gun when the deer has its head down or is looking away from you. Pick a spot just behind the shoulder and squeeze the trigger, just as you do at the range. Then, no matter what happens, sit down. Take time to calm down and then be sure to unload your rifle before you lower it down.

"Well, Son, it's up to you now. Be sure to fasten your safety belt and load your rifle carefully. Be sure to keep the hammer on half-cock until you are ready to shoot. I'll be just a ways down the ridge. If you shoot, I'll be right up. If you have trouble or need me, just holler."

The man squeezed the boy's shoulder. "Remember, Son, killing a deer isn't the most important thing this morning. Enjoy the woods and learn from them." He resisted the urge to hug his son, turned and faded into the graying darkness.

The boy took a last look around and started to climb the tree. He stopped at what he guessed was ten feet and tied off the safety belt. He tested the seat and platform and sat down. Quickly he pulled the rifle up and checked the muzzle to be sure that it was clear. With slightly trembling hands and one dropped cartridge, he loaded the magazine and levered a round into the chamber. He checked to be sure that the hammer was at half-cock and settled back against the tree.

In the dark blanket of pre-dawn, he could smell the faint hint of turpentine his father had wiped on his boots for masking scent. He listened to the calling of a horned owl and shivered a little at the slight breeze. "I wish it would hurry and get light," he thought. "Not that I'm scared or anything; it's just that I can see better in the light."

###

"The white patch suddenly moved and at once became a whole deer. The boy's breath caught, and his heart began to hammer."

###

Slowly, he began to make out the shape of the trees around him. They began to appear ghost-like out of the landscape. Then came the outlines of rocks and logs. Little by little, the white oak ridge came alive.

When it was good light, but not yet sun-up, the boy heard a rustling in the leaves. He strained his eyes and ears for another sound or a glimpse of the deer he knew must surely be coming his way. The rustling came again, closer this time. Suddenly, the boy glimpsed a flash of gray, not 20 feet from him. The squirrel jumped off the log and raced away.

The boy relaxed and smiled at himself, trying to quiet his trembling knees. He turned his attention back to the cedar thicket and trail leading to the oaks.

"Gee," he thought, "that patch of white sure looks like a deer's ear." The white patch suddenly moved and at once became a whole deer.

The boy's breath caught, and his heart hammered. Had he not been so excited, he would have better been able to study the deer. He would have seen the gleam of sunlight off the forked antlers as the buck turned its head. He would have seen the other two deer in the thicket behind the buck. Both had larger antlers.

With trembling hands and shaking knees, the boy cocked the rifle's hammer and readied himself for the shot. He tried to pick a spot behind the shoulder. The front sight began to settle in the notch of the rear sight when the gun went off.

The boy's dad fought the urge to run up the ridge. "I have to give him time to look for his deer or get his story ready," he thought. He smiled, took a fresh dip of snuff and began to slowly climb the ridge.

The boy was standing at the edge of the cedars. "Oh, Dad, I missed him." he yelled, barely able to keep the tears off his cheeks. "He was right there, and I missed him!"

His father smiled, "Son, I reckon I missed the first deer I shot at. It's nothing to be ashamed of; but before we give up, let's take a little look around. Never say you've missed a deer until you are absolutely sure."

The boy showed his dad exactly where the deer was standing. The older hunter looked back once at the stand tree, then to the boy's surprise, moved several feet farther away from the cedars. He paused, bending to look closely at the ground.

"Come here, Son," he said. "See the way the ground is all scuffed up and the way the leaves are scattered and turned over? Here's where your deer was standing. When a deer is hit, many times it will tear the ground up some. Maybe you didn't miss."

The man began to work back toward the cedars, moving slowly and studying the ground. "A hit deer will often run back the way it came. They know it is safe where they just came from," the man said. "Another thing. A deer has four legs. When they run, one of them has to hit the ground. See the way those leaves are turned over? He went that way."

"But there's no blood," said the boy.

"Even the hardest hit deer don't always bleed right away. That's why you have to really look good."

"Did I hit this deer, Dad?"

"Maybe you did and maybe you didn't," he said. "You smell anything, Son?"

"No sir."

"Sure you do," the man said. "You smell wood smoke from that house across the road. You smell the rotting leaves. You smell a hint of winter. You smell the cedars. You smell a lot of things. You just don't know how to recognize them yet.

"You see a lot, too. You see squirrels and woodpeckers, wrens, chipmunks, leaves falling and turning colors, jet vapors in the sky and beams of sunlight coming through the trees. It's all here. You just have to take time to look and learn. See, that's what deer hunting is all about. It's not just about killing a deer.

"Come here, Son. Look at that dead treetop yonder. Look close."

The boy ran to the fallen top and came to a skidding stop. The four-point had fallen just on the other side in a wide patch of sunlight. "I got him, Dad! I got him!"

This time, his dad couldn't resist a hug. As he wiped a slight bit of dew from the corner of his eye, he knew that there was another deer hunter in the family and recalled the day, many years gone, when he had killed his first deer.

Index